MW01681590

The Bible Quiz Book

www.ipibooks.com

The Bible Quiz Book

 Printed in the United States of America. Cover and interior design by Toney Mulhollan.

ISBN: 978-1-953623-70-6

About the author: Since 2003 Dr. Douglas Jacoby has been a freelance teacher and consultant. With degrees from Drew, Harvard, and Duke, Douglas has written 35 books, recorded over 1000 podcasts, and spoken in over 100 universities and in over 500 cities, in 126 nations around the world. For more information about the work, speaking schedule, and teaching ministry of Douglas Jacoby, visit his website at www.DouglasJacoby.com.

ILLUMINATION PUBLISHERS
www.ipibooks.com

Contents

Contents

Foreword

Why a Quiz Book?

"Why do we need a Bible quiz book?" Isn't it dangerous to encourage "head knowledge" without "heart knowledge"? Of course it is (1 Corinthians 8:1). But why should this book, or any other, be at odds with the goal to love the Lord our God with all our heart? Is it an either/or choice?

As Jesus relates the "greatest commandment" (Deuteronomy 6:5), he brings out its deeper meaning. In Matthew 22:37, Mark 12:30 and Luke 10:27, he adds *mind* to the equation. We are to love God with all our heart, soul, strength and mind. Well, are we doing that—loving God with all our mind?

Mathetai

Often Christians shrink from the intellectual side of the faith, and with various excuses. ("I'm too busy to read." "I have trouble concentrating." "I think prayer is more important.") But surely this is to deny our Master his right to be Lord of all, including our minds. Let's think about the word often used in the book of Acts for Christians: *disciples*. There are, in fact, many names in the Bible for a follower of Jesus Christ. *Believer, brother, saint, Christian* and *disciple* are the most common ones. Each term emphasizes a different aspect of our common experience or attitude in Christ. The word translated as disciple in the Greek New Testament is *mathetes* (mah-they-tays). What does this mean? *Mathetes* comes from the verb *manthanein*, which means "to learn." Thus, *mathetai* (plural) are learners. Since the lexicon defines disciple as "learner, student, pupil, apprentice," all these meanings are reasonable translations.

Are we learners? Some Christians think they're too old to be learners or students. And yet we see in God's word that if we aren't learners, we aren't really followers of Jesus Christ. Each one of us is called, regardless of age, gender, education or culture, to be a student. We are to be students of human nature and the world around us, persons eager to learn from anything and anyone. Above all, we are called to be avid students of the Word. Am I accurately described as a "student"? Though this isn't the only aspect of biblical Christianity that should be stressed—hopefully I am also a true believer, a loyal brother, a devoted saint and a true Christian in our mind-set—but it is certainly a fundamental one. Being a learner means that we must ask questions. It also entails being questioned, having to defend our faith.

Testing proves character. Tests solidify knowledge. Although not in an academic context, in 2 Corinthians 13:5 Paul tells his readers, "Test yourselves." (Some versions read "Examine yourselves.") To cement knowledge, fixing it into our memory so that it doesn't slip away, there is nothing like a good test!

With this in mind, *The Bible Quiz Book* has been put together. It contains 108 Bible quizzes for your learning and enjoyment. Some are only a few questions long, while the longest, *The Cosmic Bible Quiz*, contains one hundred. Questions come from every book of the Bible (all sixty-six). There's even a Time Test. (See how fast you are!)

May the Lord use this little book to sharpen our minds, whet our spiritual appetites, and draw us closer to Him.

Test yourself!
Douglas Jacoby
Marietta, Georgia

Bible Quiz 1: About Jesus Christ

❶ Jesus was Jewish: ❑ True or ❑ False?

❷ What is the incarnation of Christ?____________________

❸ When did the ascension of Christ take place?____________________

❹ What is meant by the accession of Christ? ____________________

❺ Does the Bible give us any description of the physical appearance of Christ? ____________________

❻ The earliest prophecy of the Messiah appears in which Old Testament book? ____________________

❼ Jesus never wrote a book: ❑ True or ❑ False?

❽ Jesus is mentioned by name in every book of the New Testament:

❑ True or ❑ False?

❾ In which town was Jesus born? ____________________

❿ Match the following words for Jesus with their respective languages:

Gesù	A. German	__________
Yesus	B. Polish	__________
Jezus	C. Italian	__________
Jesus	D. Indonesian	__________
Jesús	E. Spanish	__________

Answers to Bible Quiz 1: About Jesus Christ

1. Jesus was Jewish: **TRUE**

2. What is the incarnation of Christ? **THE "ENFLESHMENT" OF GOD**—God becoming man (John 1:14)

3. When did the ascension of Christ take place? **10 DAYS BEFORE PENTECOST, AND 40 DAYS AFTER THE RESURRECTION** (Luke 24, Acts 1)

4. What is meant by the accession of Christ? **HIS SITTING DOWN ON THE THRONE AT THE RIGHT HAND OF GOD**

5. Does the Bible give us any description of the physical appearance of Christ? **NO, ALTHOUGH THERE IS SOME REFERENCE IN ISAIAH TO HIS BATTERED APPEARANCE AFTER HE WAS PHYSICALLY ABUSED**

6. The earliest prophecy of the Messiah appears in which Old Testament book? **GENESIS** (See chapters 3, 24 and 49)

7. Jesus never wrote a book: **TRUE**

8. Match the following words for Jesus with their respective languages

Gesù — ITALIAN

Yesus — INDONESIAN

Jezus — POLISH

Jesus — GERMAN

Jesús — SPANISH

9. Jesus is mentioned by name in every book of the New Testament: **FALSE**. He is mentioned by name in every New Testament book except 3 John.

10. In which town was Jesus born? **BETHLEHEM**

ANSWERS

Bible Quiz 2: About the Apostle Paul

❶ Which city was Saul from? ______________________________

❷ How many letters did Paul write to individuals? ____________________

❸ Paul was a Roman citizen: ❑ True or ❑ False?

❹ From which city did Paul escape in a basket? _______________________

❺ How many chapters are there in the Corinthian letters (in all)?

____

❻ How many times was Paul shipwrecked (the minimum number)?

____

❼ Which of the following is the Spanish word for Paul?

❑ Paulo ❑ Pawel ❑ Pablo ❑ Papa

❽ Paul had only one eye: ❑ True or ❑ False?

❾ Peter and Paul had a disagreement from which they never recovered:

❑ True or ❑ False?

❿ Paul was the leader of the church universal in the first century:

❑ True or ❑ False?

Answers to Bible Quiz 2: About the Apostle Paul

1. Which city was Saul from? **TARSUS**

2. How many letters did Paul write to individuals? **FOUR** (the Pastorals plus Philemon)

3. Paul was a Roman citizen: **TRUE**

4. From which city did Paul escape in a basket? **DAMASCUS**

5. How many chapters are there in the Corinthian letters (in all)? **29**

6. How many times was Paul shipwrecked (the minimum number)? **FOUR** (2 Corinthians 11:25 plus Acts 27)

7. Which of the following is the Spanish word for Paul? **PABLO**

8. Paul had only one eye: **FALSE**

9. Peter and Paul had a disagreement from which they never recovered: **FALSE** (Compare Galatians 2:11 and 2 Peter 3:15)

10. Paul was the leader of the church universal in the first century: **FALSE**
In the first century, there was no single human leader. Both Peter and Paul had considerable spheres of influence, although neither was subordinate to the other.

ANSWERS

Bible Quiz 3: About the Apostle Peter

❶ Which relative of Peter did Jesus heal? ______________________

❷ What was Peter's other name (his Jewish name)? ______________

❸ How many letters did the apostle Peter write? ________________

❹ How many times is Peter mentioned in the Bible?

❑ 7 ❑ 57 ❑ 157 ❑ 1057

❺ Peter never truly walked on water: ❑ True or ❑ False?

❻ What was Peter's father's name? ______________________

❼ Who was his younger brother? _________________________

❽ Peter came from the fishing village of: ___________________.

❾ Cephas/Kepha is another of his names: ❑ True or ❑ False?

❿ In Greek, Peter means "rock": ❑ True or ❑ False?

Answers to Bible Quiz 3: About the Apostle Peter

1. Which relative of Peter did Jesus heal? **HIS MOTHER-IN-LAW**

2. What was Peter's other name (his Jewish name)? **SIMON OR SIMEON**

3. How many letters did the apostle Peter write? **TWO**

4. How many times is Peter mentioned in the Bible? **157**

5. Peter never truly walked on water: **FALSE**

6. What was Peter's father's name? **JONAH/JONAS/JOHN**

7. Who was his younger brother? **ANDREW**

8. Peter came from the fishing village of _________. **BETHSAIDA**

9. Cephas/Kepha is another of his names: **TRUE**

10. In Greek, Peter means "rock": **TRUE**

ANSWERS

Bible Quiz 4: The "A" List

All answers begin with the letter "A"

❶ What is the alternate name for the Book of Revelation?

____

❷ What are the extra books appearing in the Roman Catholic Old Testament called? ______________________

❸ Which son of David conspired to become king? ________________

❹ Who has been called "the fastest man in the Bible"? Hint: Genesis 2.

____

❺ Who was the husband of Prisca (Priscilla)? ________________

❻ Who, along with his wife, pretended to be more sacrificial in his giving than he really was? ________________

❼ Who was initially terrified at the prospect of sharing the gospel with Saul of Tarsus? _______________

❽ Which two books of the Bible start with the letter "A"?

____

❾ Jesus Christ is presented in scripture as the ________________ and the Omega.

❿ Who is responsible for writing at least 12 of the Psalms?

____

Answers to Bible Quiz 4: The "A" List

1. What is the alternate name for the Book of Revelation? **THE APOCALYPSE**

2. What are the extra books appearing in the Roman Catholic Old Testament called? **THE APOCRYPHA**

3. Which son of David conspired to become king? **TWO SONS, ACTUALLY: ABSALOM AND ADONIJAH**

4. Who has been called "the fastest man in the Bible"? Hint: Genesis 2. **ADAM** (He came first in the human race!)

5. Who was the husband of Prisca (Priscilla)? **AQUILA**

6. Who, along with his wife, pretended to be more sacrificial in his giving than he really was? **ANANIAS**

7. Who was initially terrified at the prospect of sharing the gospel with Saul of Tarsus? **ANANIAS** (A different fellow)

8. Which two books of the Bible start with the letter "A"? **AMOS AND ACTS**

9. Jesus Christ is presented in scripture as the ___ and the Omega. **ALPHA**

10. Who is responsible for writing at least twelve of the Psalms? **ASAPH**

ANSWERS

Bible Quiz 5: The "B" List

❶ Who was the encouraging brother who introduced Saul (Paul) to the Jerusalem apostles? ________________

❷ Matthew 22 and Luke 14 both contain parables about a ________________ .

❸ David, in his youth, killed the lion and the ________________ .

❹ What was the name of the notorious prisoner released at Passover instead of Jesus? ________________

❺ Which Old Testament city (the city from which Nebuchadnezzar ruled his empire), also becomes a symbol of the world in the book of Revelation? ____

❻ Who was the wife of Uriah the Hittite, who later became the mother of Solomon? ____

❼ Name an apostle whose name starts with "B." ________________

❽ Some people, instead of worshipping the God of the Bible, worship the Bible instead. What is the technical name for this mistake?

____

❾ Who was Jeremiah's secretary? (Archaeologists identified his seal just a few years ago!) ______________

❿ How many books of the Bible begin with "B"? ________________

Answers to Bible Quiz 5: The "B" List

1. Who was the encouraging brother who introduced Saul (Paul) to the Jerusalem apostles? **BARNABAS**

2. Matthew 22 and Luke 14 both contain parables about a ______. **BANQUET**

3. David, in his youth, killed the lion and the _____. **BEAR**

4. What was the name of the notorious prisoner released at Passover instead of Jesus? **BARABBAS**

5. Which Old Testament city (the city from which Nebuchadnezzar ruled his empire) also becomes a symbol of the world in the book of Revelation? **BABYLON**

6. Who was the wife of Uriah the Hittite, who later became the mother of Solomon? **BATHSHEBA**

7. Name an apostle whose name starts with "B." **BARTHOLOMEW**

8. Some people, instead of worshipping the God of the Bible, worship the Bible instead. What is the technical name for this mistake? **BIBLIOLATRY**

9. Who was Jeremiah's secretary? (Archaeologists identified his seal just a few years ago!) **BARUCH**

10. How many books of the Bible begin with "B"? **NONE**

ANSWERS

Bible Quiz 6: The "C" List

❶ Where did Jesus reside after Nazareth—his second home, according to the Gospels? ______________________

❷ What was the title taken by Roman Emperors in New Testament times?

____

❸ Who, in his 80s, was just as vigorous and passionate to serve God as he had been when he first entered the Promised Land as a young man?

____

❹ What is another name for the Promised Land? ____________

❺ Who was Ham's son (Noah's grandson)? ____________

❻ How many books of the Bible begin with "C"? ____________

❼ Who was the high priest when Jesus was crucified?

____

❽ Where was Barnabas from? ____________________

❾ Name one "unclean" food (Leviticus 11). ____________

❿ Who had Paul left his cloak with at Troy (Troas)?

____

Answers to Bible Quiz 6: The "C" List

1. Where did Jesus reside after Nazareth—his second home, according to the Gospels? **CAPERNAUM**

2. What was the title taken by Roman Emperors in New Testament times? **CAESAR**

3. Who, in his 80s, was just as vigorous and passionate to serve God as he had been when he first entered the Promised Land as a young man? **CALEB**

4. What is another name for the Promised Land? **CANAAN**

5. Who was Ham's son (Noah's grandson)? **CANAAN**

6. How many books of the Bible begin with "C"? **FIVE—1 AND 2 CHRONICLES, 1 AND 2 CORINTHIANS, AND COLOSSIANS**

7. Who was the high priest when Jesus was crucified? **CAIAPHAS**

8. Where was Barnabas from? **CYPRUS**

9. Name one "unclean" food (Leviticus 11). **CAMEL** (Perhaps you can find others)

10. Who had Paul left his cloak with at Troy (Troas)? **CARPUS** (2 Timothy 4:13)

ANSWERS

Bible Quiz 7: The "D" List

❶ How many books of the Old Testament begin with the letter "D"?

____

❷ How many books of the New Testament begin with "D"?

____

❸ What was the name of the Philistine corn god? ______________

❹ Who turned Samson over to the Philistines by arranging for him to have a haircut? ________________________

❺ What body of water is approximately 1,300 feet below sea level at its surface? ______________________________

❻ What is another name for the Ten Commandments?

____

❼ Who led Israel in Judges 4-5? ____________________

❽ Which of Paul's companions deserted the faith "because he loved this present world"? __________________________________

❾ Who was the "good guy" in 3 John? ______________

❿ Who was the "bad guy" in 3 John? _______________

Answers to Bible Quiz 7: The "D" List

1. How many books of the Old Testament begin with the letter "D"? **TWO: DEUTERONOMY AND DANIEL**

2. How many books of the New Testament begin with "D"? **NONE**

3. What was the name of the Philistine corn god? **DAGON**

4. Who turned Samson over to the Philistines by arranging for him to have a haircut? **DELILAH**

5. What body of water is approximately 1,300 feet below sea level at its surface? **DEAD SEA**

6. What is another name for the Ten Commandments? **DECALOGUE** (The "ten words," from the Greek)

7. Who led Israel in Judges 4-5? **DEBORAH**

8. Which of Paul's companions deserted the faith "because he loved this present world"? **DEMAS**

9. Who was the "good guy" in 3 John? **DEMETRIUS**

10. Who was the "bad guy" in 3 John? **DIOTREPHES**

ANSWERS

Bible Quiz 8: The "E" List

1. How many books of the Old Testament begin with "E"?

____

2. How many books of the New Testament begin with "E"?

____

3. Which famous garden appears early in the Bible?

____

4. Which nation became a biblical symbol for slavery and oppression?

____

5. Who miraculously fed the 100? _______________

6. Who planted the church at Colosse? _______________

7. Who was apparently the first baptism in the province of Asia?

____

8. What was the common Old Testament word for God (in Hebrew)?

____

9. Who worked alongside Nehemiah and had devoted himself to the study and observance of the Law? _______________

10. Who was the city treasurer at Corinth? _______________

Answers to Bible Quiz 8: The "E" List

1. How many books of the Old Testament begin with "E"?

FIVE: EXODUS, EZRA, ESTHER, ECCLESIASTES AND EZEKIEL

2. How many books of the New Testment begin with "E"? **ONE: EPHESIANS**

3. Which famous garden appears early in the Bible? **EDEN**

4. Which nation became a biblical symbol for slavery and oppression? **EGYPT**

5. Who miraculously fed the 100? **ELISHA**—Not as stunning as Jesus' miracles, eh?

6. Who planted the church at Colosse? **EPAPHRAS**

7. Who was apparently the first baptism in the province of Asia?

EPENETUS (Romans 16:5)

8. What was the common Old Testament word for God (in Hebrew)? **ELOHIM (ALSO EL AND ELIM)**

9. Who worked alongside Nehemiah and had devoted himself to the study and observance of the Law? **EZRA**

10. Who was the city treasurer at Corinth? **ERASTUS** (Acts 19:22, Romans 16:23, 2 Timothy 4:20).

ANSWERS

Bible Quiz 9: The "F" List

❶ In the book of Genesis, what did Joseph predict would impoverish his world? ______________________________

❷ In the book of Acts, what did Agabus predict would hit the Roman world hard? ______________________________

❸ Who preferred to send for Paul at his own convenience?

____

❹ "They devoted themselves to the apostles' teaching, to the ______________________________..."

❺ In Mark 1:16-20, what did Jesus promise to make of his disciples?

____

❻ How many years did David reign as king? ____________________

❼ What word appears in the older English Bibles to refer to premarital sex? ______________________________

❽ The Rich ____________________ was told that he would forfeit his very life that night, in a parable related by Luke.

❾ In Galatians 5, we read about nine different ____________________ ____________________ of the Spirit.

❿ Eight persons heeded God's warnings and so escaped the ____________________.

Answers to Bible Quiz 9: The "F" List

1. In the book of Genesis, what did Joseph predict would impoverish his world? **FAMINE**

2. In the book of Acts, what did Agabus predict would hit the Roman world hard? **FAMINE**

3. Who preferred to send for Paul at his own convenience? **FELIX**

4. "They devoted themselves to the apostles' teaching, to the _______..." **FELLOWSHIP**

5. In Mark 1:16-20, what did Jesus promise to make of his disciples? **FISHERS OF MEN**

6. How many years did David reign as king? **TECHNICALLY, FORTY**

7. What word appears in the older English Bibles to refer to premarital sex? **FORNICATION**

8. The Rich ________ was told that he would forfeit his very life that night, in a parable related by Luke. **FOOL**

9. In Galatians 5, we read about nine different ______ of the Spirit. **FRUIT(S)**

10. Eight persons heeded God's warnings and so escaped the _____. **FLOOD**

ANSWERS

Bible Quiz 10: The "G" List

❶ We sing, "____________________, ____________________ Hallelujah!"

❷ There is only one New Testament book beginning with "G":

❑ True or ❑ False?

❸ There is only one Old Testament book beginning with "G":

❑ True or ❑ False?

❹ "Unless a __________________ of wheat falls to the earth and dies…"

❺ Which wise Jewish teacher counseled leniency in dealing with the Christian threat? ____________________

❻ Which territory lay north of Samaria? ____________________

❼ Which language was most commonly spoken in the Roman Empire?

____

❽ What was Sodom's companion city? ____________________

❾ Where did Jesus and his disciples often meet for prayer?

____

❿ Which word appears nearly 4,400 times in the Bible?

____

Answers to Bible Quiz 10: The "G" List

1. We sing, "____, ____, Hallelujah!" **GLORY**

2. There is only one New Testament book beginning with "G": **TRUE** (Galatians)

3. There is only one Old Testament book beginning with "G": **TRUE** (Genesis)

4. "Unless a ____ of wheat falls to the earth and dies…" **GRAIN**

5. Which wise Jewish teacher counseled leniency in dealing with the Christian threat? **GAMALIEL**

6. Which territory lay north of Samaria? **GALILEE**

7. Which language was most commonly spoken in the Roman Empire? **GREEK**

8. What was Sodom's companion city? **GOMORRAH**

9. Where did Jesus and his disciples often meet for prayer? **GETHSEMANE**

10. Which word appears nearly 4,400 times in the Bible? **GOD!**

Bible Quiz 11: The "H" List

❶ This city was Abraham's home, for a while. ________________

❷ Which three Minor Prophets' names begin with "H"?

____

❸ Judas went out and ____________________ himself.

❹ What was Esther's other name? ________________

❺ Don't ________________ your brother in your heart, according to Leviticus 19:17.

❻ It's another name for the realm of the dead. ________________

❼ He was brother to Shem and Japheth. ____________________

❽ Put on the ____________________ of salvation (Ephesians 6:17).

❾ It's a musical instrument mentioned more than 25 times in the Bible—including the book of Revelation. ________________________

❿ He ordered the execution of infant boys in the region of Bethlehem no later than 4 B.C. ____

Answers to Bible Quiz 11: The "H" List

1. This city was Abraham's home, for a while. **HARAN**

2. Which three minor prophets' names begin with "H"? **HOSEA, HABAKKUK, HAGGAI**

3. Judas went out and ____ himself. **HANGED**

4. What was Esther's other name? **HADASSAH**

5. Don't ____ your brother in your heart, according to Leviticus 19:17. **HATE**

6. It's another name for the realm of the dead. **HADES**

7. He was brother to Shem and Japheth. **HAM** (and son to Noah)

8. Put on the ____ of salvation (Ephesians 6:17). **HELMET**

9. It's a musical instrument mentioned more than 25 times in the Bible—including the book of Revelation. **HARP**

10. He ordered the execution of infant boys in the region of Bethlehem no later than 4 B.C. **HEROD (THE GREAT)**

ANSWERS

Bible Quiz 12: The "I" List

❶ The largest city of the Roman Empire, with a population of more than one million, was found in which nation? ____________________

❷ Which sin is forbidden in the final verse of 1 John?

____

❸ In Hebrew, the word means "With-us God," or "God with us":

____

❹ "The perishable must clothe itself with the ____________________."

❺ The firstborn received a double share in the ____________________.

❻ To extricate himself from a tight situation, David feigned ____________________ in the presence of the Philistine king.

❼ ____________________with foreigners (non-covenant people) was strictly forbidden in the Old Testament.

❽ He was Abraham's second-born son. ____________________

❾ He was Abraham's firstborn son—although he did not receive those rights. ____________________

❿ Solomon's throne was made of gold and ____________________.

Answers to Bible Quiz 12: The "I" List

1. The largest city of the Roman Empire, with a population of more than one million, was found in which nation? **ITALY**

2. Which sin is forbidden in the final verse of 1 John? **IDOLATRY**

3. In Hebrew, the word means "With-us God," or "God with us": **IMMANUEL**

4. "The perishable must clothe itself with the ____." **IMPERISHABLE**

5. The firstborn received a double share in the _____. **INHERITANCE**

6. To extricate himself from a tight situation, David feigned _____ in the presence of the Philistine king. **INSANITY**

7. _____ with foreigners (non-covenant people) was strictly forbidden in the Old Testament. **INTERMARRIAGE**

8. He was Abraham's second-born son. **ISAAC**

9. He was Abraham's firstborn son—although he did not receive those rights. **ISHMAEL**

10. Solomon's throne was made of gold and _____. **IVORY**

Bible Quiz 13: The "J" List

❶ How many of Jesus' 12 apostles had names starting with the letter "J"?

❑ 3 ❑ 4 ❑ 5 ❑ 6

❷ What is the Hebrew letter usually transcribed as "J" in English?

❑ iota ❑ yodh ❑ jabba

❸ "Will not the ____________ of all the earth do right?" Abraham asked.

❹ He sacrificed his daughter as a burnt offering (!).__________________

❺ He suffered much at the hand of Satan, and also through his three "friends." ______________________________________

❻ It is sometimes called "Salem." __________________

❼ During his reign, the long-lost Book of the Law was discovered.

____

❽ Samson smote his enemies with a donkey's __________________.

❾ The book named after him has 52 chapters. Hint: He also wrote the Lamentations. ______________________________________

❿ The house of Simon the Tanner (Acts 10) was located in the coastal city of ____.

Answers to Bible Quiz 13: The "J" List

1. How many of Jesus' 12 apostles had names starting with the letter "J" ?

5: James and John (sons of Zebedee); James son of Alphaeus; Judas Iscariot and Judas son of James (also called Thaddaeus).

2. What is the Hebrew letter usually transcribed as "J" in English? **YODH**: Iota is Greek, and Jabba is a Hutt.

3. "Will not the _____ of all the earth do right?" Abraham asked. **JUDGE**

4. He sacrificed his daughter as a burnt offering (!). **JEPHTHAH**

5. He suffered much at the hand of Satan, and also through his three "friends." **JOB**

6. It is sometimes called "Salem." **JERUSALEM**

7. During his reign, the long-lost Book of the Law was discovered. **JOSIAH**

8. Samson smote his enemies with a donkey's _____. **JAWBONE**

9. The book named after him has 52 chapters. Hint: He also wrote the Lamentations. **JEREMIAH**

10. The house of Simon the Tanner (Acts 10) was located in the coastal city of _____. **JOPPA**

ANSWERS

Bible Quiz 14: The "K" List

1. Peter was to be given the ______________ of the kingdom of heaven.

2. He was the father of Saul (in the Old Testament). ________________

3. "Am I my brother's _______________________?" complained Cain.

4. It is the valley separating Jerusalem from the Mount of Olives.

____

5. With this, Judas betrayed the Son of Man. ______________________

6. He led a rebellion (Numbers 16). _____________________________

7. "________________________, and the door will be opened to you."

8. Levi had three sons: Gershom, Merari and ___________________.

9. The meat of the Passover meal was a lamb or a _________________.

10. This bird was one of the unclean foods in Leviticus. ______________

____

Answers to Bible Quiz 14: The "K" List

1. Peter was to be given the _____ of the kingdom of heaven. **KEYS**

2. He was the father of Saul (in the Old Testament). **KISH**

3. "Am I my brother's _____?" complained Cain. **KEEPER**

4. It is the valley separating Jerusalem from the Mount of Olives. **KIDRON**

5. With this, Judas betrayed the Son of Man. **KISS**

6. He led a rebellion (Numbers 16). **KORAH**

7. "_____, and the door will be opened to you." **KNOCK**

8. Levi had three sons: Gershom, Merari and _____. **KOHATH**

9. The meat of the Passover meal was a lamb or a _____. **KID** (a young goat)

10. This bird was one of the unclean foods in Leviticus. **KITE** (see chapter 11)

Bible Quiz 15: The "L" List

❶ He was the father of Ammon and Moab. ____________________

❷ His wife looked back and became a pillar of salt.

____

❸ Jacob worked for him more than twenty years. ____________________

❹ Jacob married her. ____________________________

❺ It's the book before Ezekiel. ____________________

❻ They were rebuked for their materialism in Revelation 3.

____

❼ Jehu turned the temple of Baal into a ___________________________.

❽ What do lamed and lambda have in common? ____________________

❾ This phrase, appearing only in Song of Songs, is rendered "faint with love" in the NIV, and "____________________" in the NAS.

❿ "____________________, come out!"

Answers to Bible Quiz 15: The "L" List

1. He was the father of Ammon and Moab. **LOT**

2. His wife looked back and became a pillar of salt. **LOT** (Yes, again!)

3. Jacob worked for him more than twenty years. **LABAN**

4. Jacob married her. **LEAH**

5. It's the book before Ezekiel. **LAMENTATIONS**

6. They were rebuked for their materialism in Revelation 3. **LAODICEA**

7. Jehu turned the temple of Baal into a _____. **LATRINE**

8. What do lamed and lambda have in common? **THE HEBREW AND GREEK LETTER "L," RESPECTIVELY**

9. This phrase, appearing only in Song of Songs, is rendered "faint with love" in the NIV, and " ____" in the NAS. **LOVESICK**

10. "_____, come out!" **LAZARUS**

Bible Quiz 16: The "M" List

❶ Who was the oldest person recorded in the Bible? ________________

❷ A vision concerning Gog and __________________ (symbolic nations representing the enemies of the people of God) came to Ezekiel.

❸ What is the meaning of "Adam"? ___________________________

❹ How many New Testament books begin with the letter "M"?

____

❺ How many Old Testament books begin with the letter "M"?

____

❻ The sons of Lot were Ammon and ___________________________.

❼ Name the high priest's servant whose ear Peter lopped off.

____

❽ He is an archangel. (His name means, literally, "Who is like God?")

____

❾ It was called "the Great Sea" in the Old Testament.

____

❿ She was the sister of Moses and Aaron. ____________________

Answers to Bible Quiz 16: The "M" List

1. Who was the oldest person in the Bible? **METHUSELAH**

2. A vision concerning Gog and ___ (symbolic nations representing the enemies of the people of God) came to Ezekiel. **MAGOG**

3. What is the meaning of "Adam"? **MAN OR MANKIND**

4. How many New Testament books begin with the letter "M"? **TWO—MATTHEW AND MARK**

5. How many Old Testament books begin with the letter "M"? **TWO—MICAH AND MALACHI**

6. The sons of Lot were Ammon and _____. **MOAB**

7. Name the high priest's servant whose ear Peter lopped off. **MALCHUS**

8. He is an archangel. (His name means, literally, "Who is like God?") **MICHAEL** (Mi = who, ke = like, el = God)

9. It was called "the Great Sea" in the Old Testament. **THE MEDITERRANEAN**

10. She was the sister of Moses and Aaron. **MIRIAM**

Bible Quiz 17: The "N" List

❶ He was a leper and the commander of the army of Syria (or Aram).

____

❷ It was Jesus' hometown. __________________________

❸ In Daniel 4, he munched grass. ______________________

❹ Jesus saw him under the sycamore-fig tree. _________________

❺ He came to Jesus at night. _____________________

❻ His son was Joshua. _____________________

❼ We brought _______________________ into the world, and we take __________________________out of it.

❽ Tough question: She was the false prophetess mentioned in the book of Nehemiah. _________________

❾ Tough question: This was the name of the priestly village on the Mount of Olives, opposite Jerusalem. _________________________

❿ Her daughter-in-law was Ruth. ____________________________

Answers to Bible Quiz 17: The "N" List

1. He was a leper and the commander of the army of Syria (Aram). **NAAMAN**

2. It was Jesus' hometown. **NAZARETH**

3. In Daniel 4, he munched grass. **NEBUCHADNEZZAR**

4. Jesus saw him under the sycamore-fig tree. **NATHANAEL**

5. He came to Jesus at night. **NICODEMUS**

6. His son was Joshua. **NUN**

7. We brought ____ into the world, and we take ____ out of it. **NOTHING!**

8. Tough question: She was the false prophetess mentioned in the book of Nehemiah. **NOADIAH**

9. Tough question: This was the name of the priestly village on the Mount of Olives, opposite Jerusalem. **NOB**

10. Her daughter-in-law was Ruth. **NAOMI**

ANSWERS

Bible Quiz 18: The "O" List

❶ A common tree in the Middle East: ____________________

❷ He was one of the Judges (and Caleb's nephew).

____

❸ He was Philemon's runaway. ____________________

❹ He is one of the minor prophets. ____________________

❺ It's the last letter of the Greek alphabet. ____________________

❻ It's the 15th letter of the Greek alphabet—and closely related to the 24th (last) letter. ____________________

❼ Absalom got his head caught in the branches of this tree.

____

❽ "They ____________________ him by the blood of the Lamb and the word of their testimony."

❾ Prophets, priests and kings were anointed with ____________________.

❿ "____________________ wide your hearts," Paul pled with the Corinthians.

Answers to Bible Quiz 18: The "O" List

1. A common tree in the Middle East. **OLIVE**

2. He was one of the Judges (and Caleb's nephew). **OTHNIEL**

3. He was Philemon's runaway. **ONESIMUS**

4. He is one of the minor prophets. **OBADIAH**

5. It's the last letter of the Greek alphabet. **OMEGA (BIG "O")**

6. It's the 15th letter of the Greek alphabet—and closely related to the 24th (last) letter. **OMICRON (LITTLE "O")**

7. Absalom got his head caught in the branches of this kind of tree. **OAK**

8. "They ____ him by the blood of the Lamb and the word of their testimony." **OVERCAME**

9. Prophets, priests and kings were anointed with ____. **OIL**

10. "____ wide your hearts," Paul pled with the Corinthians. **OPEN**

Bible Quiz 19: The "P" List

❶ It means a "comparison," and is often an earthly story containing a heavenly meaning. ______________________________

❷ It was celebrated on the 14th of Nisan. ________________

❸ This English word, featured in a recent movie, literally means "suffering." ______________________________

❹ It was the island of John's exile. ________________

❺ His old name was Saul. ______________________

❻ "When they ________________ you in one city, flee to another!"

❼ Two of the seven churches addressed in Revelation: ____________

____

❽ ______________________________ Festus succeeded Felix.

❾ It comes from the Greek word for "fifty," and on this day, many Old Testament prophecies were fulfilled. ______________________

❿ "No one who puts his hand to the ____________ and looks back…"

Answers to Bible Quiz 19: The "P" List

1. It means a "comparison," and is often an earthly story containing a heavenly meaning. **PARABLE**

2. It was celebrated on the 14th of Nisan. **PASSOVER**

3. This English word, featured in a recent film title, literally means "suffering." **PASSION**

4. It was the island of John's exile. **PATMOS**

5. His old name was Saul. **PAUL**

6. "When they ____ you in one city, flee to another!" **PERSECUTE**

7. Two of the seven churches addressed in Revelation. **PERGAMUM AND PHILADELPHIA**

8. ____ Festus succeeded Felix. **PORCIUS**

9. It comes from the Greek word for "fifty," and on this day, many Old Testament prophecies were fulfilled. **PENTECOST**

10. "No one who puts his hand to the ___ and looks back…" **PLOW**

Bible Quiz 20: The "Q" List

❶ How many books of the Bible begin with "Q"? _______________

❷ In Exodus 5, the Egyptian slave-drivers toughened the work without reducing the ________________________________.

❸ When the Israelites craved meat, the Lord sent this bird—until it "came out their nostrils"! ______________________

❹ The _______________of Sheba visited Solomon and asked him many difficult questions.

❺ Who was governor of Syria when Jesus was born? _______________

❑ Quartus ❑ Quirinius ❑ Queequeg ❑ Quadrans

❻ It is the name of the monastic community where the Dead Sea Scrolls were discovered in the 1940s and 1950s. _______________

❼ According to the evidence of archaeological discoveries, which was the national god of the nation of Edom? _______________

❑ Qarqar ❑ Qindar ❑ Qos ❑ Qaid

❽ Psalm 127 speaks of the advantages of having many sons. Solomon wrote, "Blessed is the man whose _________________ is full of them."

❾ Jude speaks of the godless persons who "are blemishes at your love feasts, eating with you without the slightest _______________, shepherds who feed only themselves."

❿ "Esau became a skillful hunter…while Jacob was a _______________ man, staying among the tents."

Answers to Bible Quiz 20: The "Q" List

1. How many books of the Bible begin with "Q"? **NONE**

2. In Exodus 5, the Egyptian slave-drivers toughened the work without reducing the ____. **QUOTA**

3. When the Israelites craved meat, the Lord sent this bird—until it "came out their nostrils"! **QUAIL**

4. The ___ of Sheba visited Solomon and asked him many difficult questions. **QUEEN**

5. Who was governor of Syria when Jesus was born? **QUIRINIUS**

6. It is the name of the monastic community where the Dead Sea Scrolls were discovered in the 1940s and 1950s. **QUMRAN**

7. According to the evidence of archaeological discoveries, which was the national god of the nation of Edom? **QOS**

8. Psalm 127 speaks of the advantages of having many sons. Solomon wrote, "Blessed is the man whose ____ is full of them." **QUIVER**

9. Jude speaks of the godless persons who "are blemishes at your love feasts, eating with you without the slightest ____, shepherds who feed only themselves." **QUALM**

10. "...Esau became a skillful hunter... while Jacob was a ______ man, staying among the tents." **QUIET**

ANSWERS

Bible Quiz 21: The "R" List

❶ She hid the spies in Jericho. ____________________

❷ Moses' father-in-law: ____________________

❸ An Aramaic term of contempt (Matthew 5): ____________________

❹ "But you are not to be called ____________________" (Matthew 23:8).

Hint: This is a title that occurs fifteen times in the New Testament.

❺ Korah's ____________________ (Numbers 16).

❻ Animal evidently sacred to the Philistines (1 Samuel 6:4):

____

❼ The Hebrew word for "wind, breath, spirit": ____________________

❑ rubba ❑ ruah ❑ raqu ❑ rupu

❽ Another name for the coney or hyrax (Leviticus 11:5):

____

❾ All the following words appear in the Bible except: ____________________

❑ robe ❑ robber ❑ ruler ❑ ring ❑ ram ❑ rape ❑ rhythm

❑ revelation ❑ route

❿ One of the requirements for salvation: ____________________

Answers to Bible Quiz 21: The "R" List

1. She hid the spies in Jericho. **RAHAB**

2. Moses' father-in-law: **REUEL**

3. An Aramaic term of contempt (Matthew 5): **RACA**

4. "But you are not to be called _____" (Matthew 23:8). Hint: This is a title that occurs fifteen times in the New Testament. **RABBI**

5. Korah's _____ (Numbers 16): **REBELLION**

6. Animal evidently sacred to the Philistines (1 Samuel 6:4): **RAT**

7. The Hebrew for "wind, breath, spirit": **RUAH**

8. Another name for the coney or hyrax (Leviticus 11:5): **ROCK BADGER**

9. All the following words appear in the Bible except: **RHYTHM**

10. One of the requirements for salvation: **REPENTANCE**

ANSWERS

Bible Quiz 22: The "S" List

❶ The seventh day of the Jewish week: ____________________

❷ What Onesimus had been (Philemon): ____________________

❸ ________________ the rod and ________________ the child.

❹ What people said who couldn't pronounce the word "shibboleth"

(Judges 12:6): ____________________________________

❺ One of the twelve tribes: __________________________

❻ The 22nd book of the Bible: ________________________

❼ Ethnicity of the bride in the 22nd book of the Bible:

____

❽ The land Paul planned to visit after visiting Rome (Romans 15):

____

❾ The "greater light" of Genesis 1: ______________________

❿ The enemy of Nehemiah: ____________________________

Answers to Bible Quiz 22: The "S" List

1. The seventh day of the Jewish week: **SABBATH**

2. What Onesimus had been (Philemon): **SLAVE**

3. ___ the rod and ___ the child. **SPARE/SPOIL**

4. What people said who couldn't pronounce the word "shibboleth" (Judges 12:6): **"SIBBOLETH"**

5. One of the twelve tribes: **SIMEON**

6. The 22nd book of the Bible: **SONG OF SONGS**

7. Ethnicity of the bride in the 22nd book of the Bible: **SHULAMMITE** (6:13)

8. The land Paul planned to visit after visiting Rome (Romans 15): **SPAIN**

9. The "greater light" of Genesis 1: **SUN**

10. The enemy of Nehemiah: **SANBALLAT**

Bible Quiz 23: The "T" List

❶ Urim and ________________ (a priestly means of ascertaining the will of God in the Old Testament)

❷ Tigers are found in the Bible: ❑ True or ❑ False?

❸ The Feast of ______________________________

❹ Paul wrote one letter to him: ___________________

❺ The New Testament Greek word for three: ❑ tria ❑ ter ❑ tres ❑ thrix

❻ Which musical instrument is found in the Bible?

❑ tuba ❑ trumpet ❑ trombone ❑ tympani

❼ "Come… see… go… _____________________" (Matthew 28:6-7).

❽ "Do not put the Lord your God to the ______________________."

❾ Paul pled with the Lord to remove his ______________ in the flesh.

❿ "Nor are you to be called ___________________" (Matthew 23:10).

Answers to Bible Quiz 23: The "T" List

1. Urim and _____ (a priestly means of ascertaining the will of God in the Old Testament) **THUMMIM**

2. Tigers are found in the Bible: **FALSE** (Lions, but no tigers)

3. The Feast of _____ **TABERNACLES**

4. Paul wrote one letter to him: **TITUS**

5. The New Testament Greek word for three: **TRIA OR TREIS**

6. Which musical instrument is found in the Bible? **TRUMPET**

7. "Come… see… go… ____" (Matthew 28:6-7). **TELL**

8. "Do not put the Lord your God to the _______." **TEST**

9. Paul pled with the Lord to remove his _____ in the flesh. **THORN**

10. "Nor are you to be called _____" (Matthew 23:10). **TEACHER**

ANSWERS

Bible Quiz 24: The "U" List

❶ ______________ and Thummim (a priestly means of ascertaining the will of God in the Old Testament)

❷ "__________________, ordinary men" (Acts 4:13, NIV)

❸ Zechariah's staffs were called Favor and ________.

❹ ______________________ the Hittite

❺ Practiced at funerals in the Middle East in biblical times (and today):

____

❻ The Last Supper took place in the Cenacle or ______________ Room.

❼ He (irreverently) tried to stabilize the Ark of the Covenant.

____

❽ City near the mouth of the Euphrates, original home of Abram's family: ____________________

❾ The southern part of Egypt (not the northern part) was called "______________________ Egypt."

❿ Charging of interest, or ________________, was forbidden under Old Testament law.

Answers to Bible Quiz 24: The "U" List

1. _____ and Thummim (a priestly means of ascertaining the will of God in the Old Testament) **URIM**

2. "_____, ordinary men" (Acts 4:13, NIV) **UNSCHOOLED**

3. Zechariah's staffs were called Favor and _____. (Zechariah 11:7) **UNION**

4. _____ the Hittite. **URIAH**

5. Practiced at funerals in the Middle East in biblical times (and today): **ULULATION** (howl or wail as an expression of strong emotion, typically grief).

6. The Last Supper took place in the Cenacle or _____ Room. **UPPER**

7. He (irreverently) tried to stabilize the Ark of the Covenant (2 Samuel 6). **UZZAH**

8. City near the mouth of the Euphrates, original home of Abram's family: **UR**

9. The southern part of Egypt (not the northern part) was called "____ Egypt." **UPPER**

10. Charging of interest, or _____, was forbidden under Old Testament law. **USURY**

Bible Quiz 25: The "V" List

❶ "Yea, though I walk through the _______________ of the shadow of death…" (KJV)

❷ She was the queen of Persian King Ahasuerus (Xerxes).

____

❸ The other name for the Hebrew letter waw: _______________

❹ The ____________________ Mary.

❺ Catholic theology distinguishes "______________" and "mortal" sins.

❻ This bird is mentioned ten times in the Bible. __________________

❼ Women generally wore the _______________ in public in Bible times.

❽ "When you make a _____________________ to God, do not delay in fulfilling it" (Ecclesiastes 5:4).

❾ The Bible has more than 30,000 of these. ____________________

❿ If one obeyed Song 2:15 (catching the little foxes) and killed them, he would technically be guilty of:

❑ vulpicide ❑ varricide ❑ vaxicide ❑ velocide

Answers to Bible Quiz 25: The "V" List

1. "Yea, though I walk through the _____ of the shadow of death…" (KJV) **VALLEY**

2. She was the queen of Persian King Ahasuerus (Xerxes). **VASHTI**

3. The other name for the Hebrew letter waw: **VAV**

4. The _____ Mary. **VIRGIN**

5. Catholic theology distinguishes "_____" and "mortal" sins. **VENIAL**

6. This bird is mentioned ten times in the Bible. **VULTURE**

7. Women generally wore the _____ in public in Bible times. **VEIL**

8. "When you make a _____ to God, do not delay in fulfilling it" (Ecclesiastes 5:4). **VOW**

9. The Bible has more than 30,000 of these. **VERSES**

10. If one obeyed Song 2:15 (catching the little foxes) and killed them, he would technically be guilty of: **VULPICIDE**

Bible Quiz 26: The "W" List

1. The usual name for an intermittent stream in the Middle East: ____________________________________

2. One of the "elements" of Communion: ____________________

3. "The ______________________ of sin is death" (Romans 6:23).

4. The other name for the Hebrew letter vav: __________________

5. Jesus made a _________________________________ of cords.

6. Vocation (?) of Rahab and Gomer: ________________________

7. They visited a little boy. ________________________________

8. He may dress in a sheepskin. _____________________________

9. "Where their ______________________________ never dies…"

10. Jacob did this until daybreak. ______________________________

Answers to Bible Quiz 26: The "W" List

1. The usual name for an intermittent stream in the Middle East: **WADI**
2. One of the "elements" of Communion: **WINE**
3. "The _____ of sin is death" (Romans 6:23). **WAGES**
4. The other name for the Hebrew letter vav: **WAW**
5. Jesus made a _____ of cords. **WHIP**
6. Vocation (?) of Rahab and Gomer: **WHORE(DOM)**
7. They visited a little boy. **WISE MEN**
8. He may dress in a sheepskin. **WOLF**
9. "Where their _____ never dies…" **WORM**
10. Jacob did this until daybreak. **WRESTLED**

ANSWERS

Bible Quiz 27: The "X" List

❶ The king of Persia mentioned thirty times in Esther and once in Daniel:

________________________________.

❷ "You shall not covet…your neighbor's ________________." (Exodus 20:17).

❸ "________________ your thoughts on Jesus" (Hebrews 3:1). "Let us ________________ our eyes on Jesus" (Hebrews 12:2).

❹ "After three months, we put out to sea in a ship that had wintered in the island. It was an Alexandrian ship with the figurehead of the twin gods Castor and ________________________" (Acts 28:11).

❺ "________________ was afraid and said, 'That's enough for now...'" (Acts 24:25).

❻ "But the __________ collector stood at a distance…" (Luke 18:13).

❼ "Go tell that ____________________…" (Jesus' message to Herod Antipas, Luke 13:32).

❽ "The ______________ is already at the root of the trees" (Luke 3:9).

❾ "A curse on him who is ________________________ in doing the Lord's work" (Jeremiah 48:10a, NIV).

❿ One of the letters of the New Testament Greek alphabet:

____

Answers to Bible Quiz 27: The "X" List

1. The king of Persia mentioned thirty times in Esther and once in Daniel: **XERXES**

2. "You shall not covet…your neighbor's _____" (Exodus 20:17). **OX**

3. "_____ your thoughts on Jesus" (Hebrews 3:1). "Let us _____ our eyes on Jesus" (Hebrews 12:2). **FIX**

4. "After three months, we put out to sea in a ship that had wintered in the island. It was an Alexandrian ship with the figurehead of the twin gods Castor and _____" (Acts 28:11). **POLLUX**

5. "_____ was afraid and said, 'That's enough for now…'" (Acts 24:25). **FELIX**

6. "But the _____ collector stood at a distance…" (Luke 18:13). **TAX**

7. "Go tell that _____..." (Jesus' message to Herod Antipas, Luke 13:32). **FOX**

8. "The _____ is already at the root of the trees" (Luke 3:9). **AX**

9. "A curse on him who is _____ in doing the Lord's work" (Jeremiah 48:10a, NIV). **LAX**

10. One of the letters of the New Testament Greek alphabet: **XI**

Bible Quiz 28: The "Y" List

❶ "Jesus Christ is the same ________________ and today and forever" (Hebrews 13:8).

❷ "Don't let anyone look down on you because you are ___________" (1 Timothy 4:12).

❸ This common pronoun appears some 13,000 times in the English Bible. ________________________________

❹ None of the following words appears in the Bible except for:

❑ yam ❑ yak ❑ yeast ❑ yahoo

❺ Which of the following begins with a "Y" sound in the original Hebrew? ❑ Moses ❑ Judah ❑ Haman ❑ Arabah

❻ How many books of the Bible begin with the letter "Y"?

____

❼ God's covenant name in the Old Testament: ______________

❽ "In the 480th ___________ after the Israelites had come out of Egypt…" (1 Kings 6:1).

❾ How else can the personal name Syzygus (Philippians 4:3) be translated? ______________________

❿ "For no matter how many promises God has made, they are ________________________ in Christ" (2 Corinthians 1:20).

Answers to Bible Quiz 28: The "Y" List

1. "Jesus Christ is the same ____ and today and forever" (Hebrews 13:8).

YESTERDAY

2. "Don't let anyone look down on you because you are _____" (1 Timothy 4:12).

YOUNG

3. This common pronoun appears some 13,000 times in the English Bible. **YOU**

4. None of the following words appears in the Bible except for: **YEAST**

5. Which of the following begins with a "Y" sound in the original Hebrew?

JUDAH

6. How many books of the Bible begin with the letter "Y"? **NONE**

7. God's covenant name in the Old Testament: **YAHWEH**

8. "In the 480th _____ after the Israelites had come out of Egypt..." (1 Kings 6:1)

YEAR

9. How else can the personal name Syzygus (Philippians 4:3) be translated?

YOKEFELLOW

10. "For no matter how many promises God has made, they are _____ in Christ" (2 Corinthians 1:20). **YES**

Bible Quiz 29: The "Z" List

❶ He was governor of Judah in Haggai 1:14. _______________

❷ One of the deserts in which the Israelites spent their forty years wandering: ___________

❸ Another name for Jerusalem: ______________________________

❹ Several years after the birth of Christ, this is the year that never was.

____

❺ He was king of northern Israel for a whopping seven days (1 Kings 16:15)! ____

❻ Another name for the Rephaites (Deuteronomy 2:20): _____________

❼ In Numbers 26, 27 and 36, this man had only daughters, and it was legislated that they would receive an inheritance. _______________

❽ Name the two minor prophets whose names begin with "Z."

____

❾ The Philistine city given to David when he was on the run from Saul:

____

❿ He was the father of James and John. _______________________

Answers to Bible Quiz 29: The "Z" List

1. He was governor of Judah in Haggai 1:14. **ZERUBBABEL**

2. One of the deserts in which the Israelites spent their forty years wandering: **ZIN**

3. Another name for Jerusalem: **ZION**

4. Several years after the birth of Christ, this is the year that never was. **ZERO**

5. He was king of northern Israel for a whopping seven days (1 Kings 16:15)! **ZIMRI**

6. Another name for the Rephaites (Deuteronomy 2:20): **ZAMZUMMIM / ZAMZUMMITES**

7. In Numbers 26, 27 and 36, this man had only daughters, and it was legislated that they would receive an inheritance. **ZELOPHEHAD**

8. Name the two minor prophets whose names begin with "Z." **ZEPHANIAH AND ZECHARIAH**

9. The Philistine city given to David when he was on the run from Saul: **ZIKLAG**

10. He was the father of James and John. **ZEBEDEE**

Bible Quiz 30: Genesis

❶ His name also means "mankind." ____________________

❷ Name Cain's two brothers. ____________________

❸ Where was the enormous tower built—which the Lord opposed, because people were more interested in making a name for themselves than in glorifying him? ____________________

❹ How many chapters does Genesis have? ❑ 30 ❑ 40 ❑ 50 ❑ 60

❺ What language was Genesis written in? ____________________

❻ What other language—comprising 3% of the Old Testament—is found in a single verse of Genesis? ____________________

❼ How long was Noah's Ark? ❑ 150 ft. ❑ 450 ft. ❑ 1050 ft. ❑ 1750 ft.

❽ Which of the following characters does not appear in Genesis?

❑ Abraham ❑ Goliath ❑ Ishmael ❑ Joseph

❾ How many sons did Jacob have? ____________________

❿ Which New Testament book starts with the same three words that Genesis begins with? ____________________

Answers to Bible Quiz 30: Genesis

1. His name also means “mankind.” **ADAM**

2. Name Cain’s two brothers. **ABEL AND SETH**

3. Where was the enormous tower built—which the Lord opposed, because people were more interested in making a name for themselves than in glorifying him? **BABEL**

4. How many chapters does Genesis have? **50**

5. What language was Genesis written in? **HEBREW**

6. What other language—comprising 3% of the Old Testament—is found in a single verse of Genesis? **ARAMAIC**

7. How long was Noah’s Ark? **450 FEET**

8. Which of the following characters does not appear in Genesis? **GOLIATH**

9. How many sons did Jacob have? **12**

10. Which New Testament book starts with the same three words that Genesis begins with? **JOHN** (“In the beginning…”)

Bible Quiz 31: Exodus

❶ Who is the central figure of Exodus? ____________________

❷ How many chapters are in the book? ❑ 20 ❑ 40 ❑ 60 ❑ 80

❸ Who led Egypt? ____________________

❹ Finally, at the end of the book, the ____________________ has been constructed.

❺ Who is Zipporah? ____________________

❻ What was Jethro's advice in Exodus 18? ____________________

____

❼ In which chapter do we find the apostasy in connection with the golden calves? ❑ 2 ❑ 12 ❑ 22 ❑ 32

❽ Who were Shiphrah and Puah? ____________________

❾ In which chapter do we find the Ten Commandments? ____________

❿ Which book follows Exodus? ____________________

Answers to Bible Quiz 31: Exodus

1. Who is the central figure of Exodus? **MOSES**

2. How many chapters are in the book? **40**

3. Who led Egypt? **PHARAOH**

4. Finally, at the end of the book, the ____ has been constructed. **TABERNACLE**

5. Who is Zipporah? **MOSES' WIFE**

6. What was Jethro's advice in Exodus 18? **SLOW DOWN—DELEGATE!**

7. In which chapter do we find the apostasy in connection with the golden calves? **32**

8. Who were Shiphrah and Puah? **THE HEBREW MIDWIVES**

9. In which chapter do we find the Ten Commandments? **20**

10. Which book follows Exodus? **LEVITICUS**

Bible Quiz 32: Leviticus

❶ This book is named "Leviticus" after the priestly Levites whose responsibility it was to superintend the Tabernacle and the sacrifices:

❑ True or ❑ False?

❷ The book has 27 chapters and precedes Deuteronomy:

❑ True or ❑ False?

❸ Nadab and Abihu are struck dead in chapter: ❑ 1 ❑ 10 ❑ 20 ❑ 30

❹ Blood and fat are acceptable foods for Israelites, according to Leviticus: ❑ True or ❑ False?

❺ The Levites diagnosed mildew and skin diseases: ❑ True or ❑ False?

❻ "Love your neighbor as yourself" appears in this book:

❑ True or ❑ False?

❼ According to 20:13, sodomy merits the ______________________.

❽ The chapter that predicts blessings (or disasters) depending on Israel's obedience (or disobedience) is chapter: ❑ 6 ❑ 16 ❑ 26 ❑ 66

❾ Chapter 25 contains instructions concerning the Year of Jubilee:

❑ True or ❑ False?

❿ The "keyword" in Leviticus is: ❑ happy ❑ holy ❑ humane ❑ holistic

Answers to Bible Quiz 32: Leviticus

1. This book is named “Leviticus” after the priestly Levites whose responsibility it was to superintend the Tabernacle and the sacrifices. **TRUE**

2. The book has 27 chapters and precedes Deuteronomy: **TRUE** (it immediately precedes Numbers, but it still—technically speaking—comes before Deuteronomy)

3. Nadab and Abihu are struck dead in chapter: **10.**

4. Blood and fat are acceptable foods for Israelites, according to Leviticus: **FALSE**

5. The Levites diagnosed mildew and skin diseases: **TRUE (!)**

6. “Love your neighbor as yourself” appears in this book: **TRUE**

7. According to 20:13, sodomy merits the _____. **DEATH PENALTY**

8. The chapter that predicts blessings (or disasters) depending on Israel’s obedience (or disobedience) is chapter: **26**

9. Chapter 25 contains instructions concerning the Year of Jubilee: **TRUE**

10. The “keyword” in Leviticus is: **HOLY**

Bible Quiz 33: Numbers

❶ The book of Numbers is set in:

❑ Egypt ❑ The Desert ❑ Canaan ❑ Israel

❷ How many chapters are there in Numbers? ❑ 16 ❑ 26 ❑ 36 ❑ 46

❸ Numbers 12 tells us that God normally spoke to the prophets through:

❑ crystal balls ❑ dreams ❑ mystical sensations ❑ Urim and Thummim

❹ How many censuses are recorded in this book? ________________

❺ Which book precedes Numbers? ____________________________

❻ Who led a rebellion against Moses and Aaron?

❑ Korah ❑ Konan ❑ Kenan ❑ Kabzeel

❼ The Nazirite vow is found in this book: ❑ True or ❑ False?

❽ The so-called priestly blessing ("The Lord bless you and keep you") appears in Numbers chapter: ❑ 5 ❑ 6 ❑ 22 ❑ 37

❾ The silver trumpets (Numbers 10) were used for which purpose(s):

❑ To convene leaders' meetings

❑ To signal that it was a time for Israel to break camp

❑ For musical entertainment

❿ When Moses strikes the rock, in direct opposition to God's instructions, the much-desired water does not flow forth from it:

❑ True or ❑ False?

Answers to Bible Quiz 33: Numbers

1. The book of Numbers is set in: **THE DESERT**

2. How many chapters are there in Numbers? **36**

3. Numbers 12 tells us that God normally spoke to the prophets through: **DREAMS**

4. How many censuses are recorded in this book? **TWO**

5. Which book precedes numbers? **LEVITICUS**

6. Who led a rebellion against Moses and Aaron? **KORAH**

7. The Nazirite vow is found in this book: **TRUE**

8. The so-called priestly blessing ("The Lord bless you and keep you") appears in Numbers chapter: **6**

9. The silver trumpets (Numbers 10) were used for which purpose(s): **BOTH TO CONVENE LEADERS' MEETINGS AND TO SIGNAL A TIME FOR ISRAEL TO BREAK CAMP.**

10. Since Moses struck the rock, in direct opposition to God's instructions, the much-desired water did not flow forth from it. **FALSE**

ANSWERS

Bible Quiz 34: Deuteronomy

❶ Deuteronomy is the ________________ book of the Bible.

❑ 4th ❑ 5th ❑ 6th ❑ 7th

❷ In which chapter do we find the Decalogue? ________________

❸ The death of Moses is recorded in chapter: ❑ 33 ❑ 34 ❑ 35 ❑ 36

❹ Deuteronomy is the most quoted book of the Torah in the New Testament: ❑ True or ❑ False?

❺ Deuteronomy 15:1 reads, "At the end of every seven years you must cancel ____________________."

❻ According to Acts 3, a prophet like Moses was to be raised up. That person was none other than ________________.

❼ Chapter 21 reads, "If a man guilty of a capital offense is put to death and his body is hung on a tree, you must not leave his body on the tree ____."

❽ Deuteronomy 23:15 says that a runaway slave must not be returned to his master. Did Paul feel obligated to follow this precept in the situation involving Onesimus and Philemon? ________________________

❾ Chapter 25 reads, "Do not __________________ an ox while it is treading out the grain."

❿ The book of Deuteronomy, largely a review of the wilderness wanderings, begins at the end of which year since the exodus?

____

Answers to Bible Quiz 34: Deuteronomy

1. Deuteronomy is the ____ book of the Bible: **5TH**

2. In which chapter do we find the Decalogue? **5TH**

3. The death of Moses is recorded in chapter: **34**

4. Deuteronomy is the most quoted book of the Torah in the New Testament: **TRUE**

5. Deuteronomy 15:1 reads, "At the end of every seven years you must cancel _____." **DEBTS**

6. According to Acts 3, a prophet like Moses was to be raised up. That person was none other than _____. **JESUS CHRIST**

7. Chapter 21 reads, "If a man guilty of a capital offense is put to death and his body is hung on a tree, you must not leave his body on the tree _____." **OVERNIGHT**

8. Deuteronomy 23:15 says that a runaway slave must not be returned to his master. Did Paul feel obligated to follow this precept in the situation involving Onesimus and Philemon? **NO**

9. Chapter 25 reads, "Do not _____ an ox while it is treading out the grain." **MUZZLE**

10. The book of Deuteronomy, largely a review of the wilderness wanderings, begins at the end of which year since the exodus? **FORTIETH (THE FINAL YEAR)**

Bible Quiz 35: Joshua

❶ What is Joshua's other name? ______________________________

❷ Joshua was one of the twelve spies: ❑ True or ❑ False?

❸ According to Deuteronomy 34:9, "Now Joshua son of Nun was filled with _____________________ because Moses had laid his hands on him. So the Israelites listened to him and did what the LORD had commanded Moses."

❹ What was the first city to fall in the Conquest? __________________

❺ Which came first, the southern campaign or the northern campaign?

____

❻ Who said, "As for me and my household, we will serve the Lord"?

____

❼ What was Joshua's age at his death? ❑ 90 ❑ 110 ❑ 130 ❑ 150

❽ The first attack against the city of Ai was successful:

❑ True or ❑ False?

❾ Who pretended to be a distant people, rather than Canaanites, in order to avoid being attacked by Israel?

❑ Jebusites ❑ Gibeonites ❑ Hittites ❑ Marmites

❿ Before he died, the Lord repeatedly told Joshua, "Be strong and

_____________________________."

Answers to Bible Quiz 35: Joshua

1. What is Joshua's other name? **HOSHEA (13:16)**

2. Joshua was one of the twelve spies: **TRUE**

3. According to Deuteronomy 34:9, "Now Joshua son of Nun was filled with _____ because Moses had laid his hands on him. So the Israelites listened to him and did what the LORD had commanded Moses."

THE SPIRIT OF WISDOM

4. What was the first city to fall in the Conquest? **JERICHO**

5. Which came first, the southern campaign or the northern campaign?

SOUTHERN

6. Who said, "As for me and my household, we will serve the Lord"? **JOSHUA**

7. What was Joshua's age at his death? **110**

8. The first attack against the city of Ai was successful: **FALSE**

9. Who pretended to be a distant people, rather than Canaanites, in order to avoid being attacked by Israel? **GIBEONITES**

10. Before he died, the Lord repeatedly told Joshua, "Be strong and _____."

COURAGEOUS

Bible Quiz 36: Judges

❶ Which book comes before Judges? ______________________

❷ Each judge led all the tribes of Israel when he/she judged:

❑ True or ❑ False?

❸ Who was the strong man with a weakness for women?

____

❹ Who defeated the Midianites, though vastly outnumbered?

____

❺ Who sacrificed his own daughter as a burnt offering in fulfillment of a vow? ____

❻ Who was the first judge of Israel? ________________________

❼ How many chapters are there in Judges? __________________

❽ Which judge assassinated the grossly obese Eglon, the Moabite oppressor of Israel? ________________________________

❾ Place the following significant women from the book of Judges in the order of their first mention: ❑ Delilah ❑ Deborah ❑ Jael ❑ Jephthah's daughter: ____

❿ Which of the following is the final verse of the book? ___________

❑ Then Samson prayed to the LORD, "O Sovereign LORD, remember me. O God, please strengthen me just once more, and let me with one blow get revenge on the Philistines for my two eyes."

❑ "But grant me this one request," she said. "Give me two months to roam the hills and weep with my friends, because I will never marry."

❑ In those days, Israel had no king; everyone did as he saw fit.

❑ After the death of Joshua, the Israelites asked the LORD, "Who will be the first to go up and fight for us against the Canaanites?"

Answers to Bible Quiz 36: Judges

1. Which book comes before Judges? **JOSHUA**

2. Each judge led all the tribes of Israel when he/she judged: **FALSE**

Each judge led several tribes, not all Israel.

3. Who was the strong man with a weakness for women? **SAMSON**

4. Who defeated the Midianites, though vastly outnumbered? **GIDEON**

5. Who sacrificed his own daughter as a burnt offering in fulfillment of a vow?

JEPHTHAH

6. Who was the first judge of Israel? **OTHNIEL**

7. How many chapters are there in Judges? **21**

8. Which judge assassinated the grossly obese Eglon, the Moabite oppressor of Israel?

EHUD

9. Place the following significant women from the book of Judges in the order of their first mention:

DEBORAH, JAEL, JEPHTHAH'S DAUGHTER, DELILAH

10. What of the following is the final verse of the book?

IN THOSE DAYS, ISRAEL HAD NO KING; EVERYONE DID AS HE SAW FIT. (21:25)

Bible Quiz 37: Ruth

❶ The Dead Sea Scrolls include no manuscripts of Ruth:

❑ True or ❑ False?

❷ Ruth's family fled to Moab from the famine that was ravaging Israel:

❑ True or ❑ False?

❸ Which book of the Bible comes after Ruth? ____________________

❹ In how many books of the Bible is Ruth mentioned? _____________

❺ How many chapters does this short book contain? ______________

❻ Name Ruth's mother-in-law. _______________________________

❼ About how many years did Ruth's mother-in-law live in Moab?

❑ 10 ❑ 20 ❑ 30 ❑ 40

❽ To what city did Ruth return from Moab, after the death of her husband? ____

❾ Whom did the widow Ruth marry? ____________________

❿ Who were Ruth's two most illustrious descendants?

____

Answers to Bible Quiz 37: Ruth

1. The Dead Sea Scrolls include no manuscripts of Ruth: **FALSE**

Every book of the Bible is represented, with the possible exception of Esther.

2. Ruth's family fled to Moab from the famine that was ravaging Israel: **FALSE**

It was Naomi's family that fled; Ruth was already in Moab.

3. Which book of the Bible comes after Ruth? **1 SAMUEL**

4. In how many books of the Bible is Ruth mentioned? **ONLY 2:** Ruth and Matthew

5. How many chapters does this short book contain? **FOUR**

6. Name Ruth's mother-in-law. **NAOMI**

7. About how many years did Ruth's mother-in-law live in Moab? **10**

8. To what city did Ruth return from Moab, after the death of her husband? **BETHLEHEM**

9. Whom did the widow Ruth marry? **BOAZ**

10. Who were Ruth's two most illustrious descendants? **DAVID AND JESUS CHRIST**

Bible Quiz 38: 1 and 2 Samuel

❶ In what capacity did Samuel serve Israel?

❑ Prophet ❑ King ❑ Priest ❑ Military commander

❷ Which book comes after 2 Samuel? ____________________________

❸ Samuel was alive at the beginning of 1 Samuel, and lived all the way until the end of 2 Samuel: ❑ True or ❑ False?

❹ Who were typically the enemies of Israel in 1-2 Samuel?____________

❺ How many chapters are in 1 and 2 Samuel (combined)?

❑ 40 ❑ 55 ❑ 65 ❑ 80

❻ Which king of Israel died at the end of 1 Samuel? __________________

❼ Which character is not mentioned in 1-2 Samuel?

❑ Hannah ❑ Goliath ❑ Absalom ❑ Caleb ❑ Solomon

❽ Who consulted a witch (a medium) in 1 Samuel 28? ________________

❾ Who was Joab? ____________________________

❿ Who feigned insanity in the presence of Achish, king of Gath?

____

Answers to Bible Quiz 38: 1 and 2 Samuel

1. In what capacity did Samuel serve Israel? **PROPHET AND PRIEST.** Samuel served as priest and prophet. Interestingly, as leader of Israel, he fulfilled (in some ways) the function of king. He was not a military commander.

2. Which book comes after 2 Samuel? **1 KINGS**

3. Samuel was alive at the beginning of 1 Samuel, and lived all the way until the end of 2 Samuel: **FALSE.** Although he was born in 1 Samuel 1, he died in 1 Samuel 25. He is not alive in 2 Samuel at all.

4. Who were typically the enemies of Israel in 1-2 Samuel? **THE PHILISTINES**

5. How many chapters are in 1 and 2 Samuel (combined)? **55**

6. Which king of Israel died at the end of 1 Samuel? **SAUL**

7. Which character is not mentioned in 1-2 Samuel? **CALEB**

8. Who consulted a witch (a medium) in 1 Samuel 28? **SAUL**

9. Who was Joab? **DAVID'S ARMY COMMANDER**

10. Who feigned insanity in the presence of Achish, king of Gath? **DAVID**

Bible Quiz 39: 1 and 2 Kings

❶ Despite a foiled coup d'etat, who takes the throne at the beginning of 1 Kings? ____

❷ What was the initial leadership style of his son and successor? What happened as a result? ____________________________________

____

❸ The Northern Kingdom officially (and separately) began around 931 B.C. In which chapter do we read of this development?

❑ 1 Kings 31 ❑ 1 Kings 12 ❑ 1 Kings 29 ❑ 2 Kings 5

❹ How did Hiram help Solomon? _______________

❺ Elijah is mentioned in 1 Kings: ❑ True or ❑ False?

❻ Elisha is mentioned in 1 Kings: ❑ True or ❑ False?

❼ Who arranged the death of Naboth so that Ahab could seize his property? ____

❽ Which king and commander slaughtered the Baal worshipers? ______

____

❾ How does 2 Kings end?

❑ The Assyrians overrun Northern Israel.

❑ The Babylonians destroy Jerusalem and take Judah captive.

❑ Josiah's men find the long-lost Book of the Law.

❑ None of the above.

❿ Who were the perennial enemies of Israel in these books?

____

Answers to Bible Quiz 39: 1 and 2 Kings

1. Despite a foiled coup d'etat, who takes the throne at the beginning of 1 Kings? **SOLOMON**

2. What was the initial leadership style of his son and successor? What happened as a result? **HARSH! PEOPLE WERE DISHEARTENED, AND THIS LED TO ISRAEL DIVIDING INTO TWO NATIONS.**

3. The Northern Kingdom officially (and separately) began around 931 B.C. In which chapter do we read of this development? **1 KINGS 12**

4. How did Hiram help Solomon? **HE PROVIDED MATERIALS FOR CONSTRUCTION OF THE TEMPLE**

5. Elijah is mentioned in 1 Kings: **TRUE**

6. Elisha is mentioned in 1 Kings: **TRUE**

7. Who arranged the death of Naboth so that Ahab could seize his property? **QUEEN JEZEBEL**

8. Which king and commander slaughtered the Baal worshipers? **JEHU**

9. How does 2 Kings end? **THE BABYLONIANS DESTROY JERUSALEM AND TAKE JUDAH CAPTIVE.**

10. Who were the perennial enemies of Israel in these books? **THE ARAMEANS (SYRIANS)**

Bible Quiz 40: 1 and 2 Chronicles

❶ Whereas 1-2 Kings focuses on the history of Northern Israel and Southern Judah, 1-2 Chronicles focuses primarily on:

❑ Northern Israel ❑ Southern Judah ❑ Egypt ❑ Assyria

❷ What is the first word of 1 Chronicles?

❑ David ❑ Adam ❑ Seth ❑ The

❸ Who succeeds David as king at the end of 1 Chronicles?

____

❹ How many chapters are there in 1-2 Chronicles?

❑ 55 ❑ 65 ❑ 75 ❑ 85

❺ Chronicles was the last book of the Hebrew Old Testament:

❑ True or ❑ False?

❻ Who destroyed Jerusalem at the end of the 2 Chronicles?

____

❼ In the last three verses of 2 Chronicles, seventy years elapse and a decree is made. What is the decree? ____________________

____

❽ In 2 Chronicles 26, King Uzziah becomes "incensed" when challenged by eighty priests. What specifically did they challenge him about?

____

❾ What book follows 2 Chronicles in most modern Bibles?

____

❿ Who requests wisdom in the first chapter of 2 Chronicles? Hint: The parallel account is found in 1 Kings 3. ____________________

Answers to Bible Quiz 40: 1 and 2 Chronicles

1. Whereas 1-2 Kings focuses on the history of Northern Israel and Southern Judah, 1-2 Chronicles focuses primarily on: **SOUTHERN UDAH**

2. What is the first word of 1 Chronicles? **ADAM**

3. Who succeeds David as king at the end of 1 Chronicles? **SOLOMON**

4. How many chapters are there in 1-2 Chronicles? **65** (29+36)

5. Chronicles was the last book of the Hebrew Old Testament: **TRUE**

6. Who destroyed Jerusalem at the end of the 2 Chronicles?
THE BABYLONIANS (or, more specifically, Nebuchadnezzar)

7. In the last three verses of 2 Chronicles, seventy years elapse and a decree is made. What is the decree? **THE TEMPLE WILL BE REBUILT, AND THE JEWS MAY RETURN TO THEIR LAND**

8. In 2 Chronicles 26, King Uzziah becomes "incensed" when challenged by eighty priests. What specifically did they challenge him about?
HE ARROGANTLY OFFERED INCENSE IN THE TEMPLE, EVEN THOUGH HE WAS NOT A PRIEST.

9. What book follows 2 Chronicles in most modern Bibles? **EZRA**

10. Who requests wisdom in the first chapter of 2 Chronicles? Hint: The parallel account is found in 1 Kings 3. **SOLOMON**

ANSWERS

Bible Quiz 41: Ezra-Nehemiah

❶ Which of these two books concerns rebuilding the walls of Jerusalem?

____

❷ Which book concerns rebuilding the Temple? ______________

❸ Nehemiah was a priest: ❑ True or ❑ False?

❹ Ezra was cupbearer to King Artaxerxes: ❑ True or ❑ False?

❺ Sanballat was the Samaritan enemy of the builders, and his existence and position as governor has been proved archaeologically. How many times is he mentioned in Nehemiah? ❑ 7 ❑ 10 ❑ 22 ❑ 33

❻ During the Exile, the Jews were unfaithful to God by marrying outside the faith. This is recorded in: ❑ Ezra ❑ Nehemiah ❑ Neither ❑ Both

❼ The wall was completed in: ❑ 1 day ❑ 7 weeks ❑ 52 days ❑ 70 years

❽ How long did Ezra read from the book of the Law by the Water Gate?

❑ 1 hour ❑ 3 hours ❑ 6 hours ❑ 12 hours

❾ How many chapters in all are in these two books (sometimes counted as a single book by the ancient Jews): ❑ 13 ❑ 23 ❑ 33 ❑ 43

❿ In which century are these two books set? ______________

Answers to Bible Quiz 41: Ezra-Nehemiah

1. Which of these two books concerns rebuilding the walls of Jerusalem? **NEHEMIAH**

2. Which book concerns rebuilding the Temple? **EZRA**

3. Nehemiah was a priest: **FALSE**

4. Ezra was cupbearer to King Artaxerxes: **FALSE**

5. Sanballat was the Samaritan enemy of the builders, and his existence and position as governor has been proved archaeologically. How many times is he mentioned in Nehemiah? **10**

6. During the Exile, the Jews were unfaithful to God by marrying outside the faith. This is recorded in: **BOTH**

7. The wall was completed in: **52 DAYS**

8. How long did Ezra read from the book of the Law by the Water Gate? **6 HOURS**

9. How many chapters in all are in these two books (sometimes counted as a single book by the ancient Jews)? **23**

10. In which century are these two books set? **THE 5TH CENTURY B.C.** (the 400s)

Bible Quiz 42: Esther

❶ Whom did Esther "replace"? ______________________

❷ What was her Jewish (Hebrew) name (which means "beautiful")?

____

❸ Who was her husband? ______________________

❹ Where did he live? ❑ Susa ❑ Ecbatana ❑ Tehran ❑ Casiphia

❺ Who had adopted her and protected her all her life?

____

❻ Who tried to kill this person and was eventually hanged on a gallow?

____

❼ Which Jewish holiday derives from this fifth-century near-holocaust?

____

❽ How many chapters does Esther have? ______________________

❾ Which book follows Esther? ______________________

❿ How did Esther save her people? ______________________

Answers to Bible Quiz 42: Esther

1. Whom did Esther "replace"? **VASHTI**

2. What was her Jewish (Hebrew) name (which means "beautiful")?

HADASSAH

3. Who was her husband? **XERXES**

4. Where did he live? **SUSA**

5. Who had adopted her and protected her all her life? **MORDECAI**

6. Who tried to kill this person and was eventually hanged on a gallow?

HAMAN

7. Which Jewish holiday derives from this fifth-century near-holocaust?

PURIM

8. How many chapters does Esther have? **10**

9. Which book follows Esther? **JOB**

10. How did Esther save her people?

SHE ASKED THE KING TO STOP THE PROPOSED GENOCIDE

Bible Quiz 43: Job

❶ Where did Job live?

❑ Israel ❑ Uz ❑ Egypt ❑ Anatolia

❷ Who are Eliphaz, Bildad and Zophar? ___________________

❸ Job called these men "miserable comforters" and "worthless

____."

❹ Job lost all his close relations except for ___________________.

❺ Who (apparently) was the youngest of the five primary human

speakers in Job? ____

❻ Whom did God allow to test and hurt Job? ___________________

❼ Which books is Job mentioned in? Hint: There is one Old Testament

book (besides Job) and one New Testament book. ___________________

❽ Who rebukes Job from the storm (whirlwind)? ___________________

❾ Who was Jemimah? ____

❿ What is the theological error the book of Job refutes?

____

Answers to Bible Quiz 43: Job

1. Where did Job live? **UZ**

2. Who are Eliphaz, Bildad, and Zophar? **HIS FRIENDS**

3. Job called these men "miserable comforters" and "worthless _____".

PHYSICIANS

4. Job lost all his close relations except for: **HIS WIFE**

5. Who (apparently) was the youngest of the five primary human speakers in Job?

ELIHU

6. Whom did God allow to test and hurt Job? **SATAN**

7. Which books is Job mentioned in? Hint: There is one Old Testament book (besides Job) and one New Testament book. **EZEKIEL AND JAMES**

8. Who rebukes Job from the storm (whirlwind)? **GOD**

9. Who was Jemimah? **ONE OF JOB'S DAUGHTERS** (Chapter 42)

10. What is the theological error the book of Job refutes?

THAT BAD THINGS ONLY HAPPEN TO BAD PEOPLE/GOOD THINGS HAPPEN TO GOOD PEOPLE (PROSPERITY THEOLOGY)

Bible Quiz 44: Psalms

❶ How many Psalms are there in the book of Psalms? _______________

❷ Psalms were originally intended to be sung to a percussion instrument:

❑ True or ❑ False?

❸ Which book follows Psalms? __________________________________

❹ Psalm 151 is which of the following?

❑ Nonexistent ❑ Apocryphal ❑ Canonical ❑ In the New Testament

❺ Which psalm(s) describe two ways and two kinds of people?

❑ 1 ❑ 19 and 119 ❑ 88 ❑ 117

❻ In which psalm(s) does the psalmist cry, "The darkness is my closest friend"? ❑ 1 ❑ 19 and 119 ❑ 88 ❑ 117

❼ Which psalm(s) expresses a vision for all nations to come to know God?

❑ 1 ❑ 19 and 119 ❑ 88 ❑ 117

❽ Which psalm(s) extols the wonders of the word of God?

❑ 1 ❑ 19 and 119 ❑ 88 ❑ 117

❾ Which is the longest acrostic psalm in the psalter? ________________

❿ The "sin psalms" include all the following except:

❑ Psalm 32 ❑ Psalm 38 ❑ Psalm 51 ❑ Psalm 118

Answers to Bible Quiz 44: Psalms

1. How many psalms are there in the book of Psalms? **150**

2. Psalms were originally intended to be sung to a percussion instrument: **FALSE**

They were sung to stringed instruments.

3. Which book follows Psalms? **PROVERBS**

4. Psalm 151 is which of the following: **APOCRYPHAL**

Although it does not properly belong in the canon, it does occasionally appear in some Bibles.

5. Which psalm(s) describes two ways and two kinds of people? **1**

6. In which psalm(s) does the psalmist cry, "The darkness is my closest friend"? **88**

7. Which psalm(s) expresses a vision for all nations to come to know God? **117**

8. Which psalm(s) extols the wonders of the word of God? **19 AND 119**

9. Which is the longest acrostic psalm in the psalter? **PSALM 117**

10. The "sin psalms" include all the following except: **PSALM 118**

Bible Quiz 45: Proverbs

❶ Who is credited with writing (most of) the Proverbs? ____________

❷ Which three chapters deal with avoiding the adulteress?

❑ 1-3 ❑ 5-7 ❑ 15-17 ❑ 21-23

❸ In which chapter does the Woman of Noble Character appear?

____

❹ In which chapter do we read that good news from a distant land is like cool water to the soul? ________________________

❺ "The guilty flee when none pursue" is found in chapter:

❑ 8 ❑ 18 ❑ 28 ❑ 38

❻ "The fear of the Lord is the beginning of ________________."

❼ "As ________________ sharpens ________________, so one man sharpens another."

❽ "Do not add to his words, or he will rebuke you and prove you a liar" is found in: ❑ 10:6 ❑ 20:6 ❑ 30:6 ❑ 33:6

❾ Which book follows Proverbs? ________________________

❿ Proverbs 13:24 reads, "He who spares the rod ________________ his son."

Answers to Bible Quiz 45: Proverbs

1. Who is credited with writing (most of) the Proverbs? **SOLOMON**

2. Which three chapters deal with avoiding the adulteress? **5-7**

3. In which chapter does the Woman of Noble Character appear? **31**

4. In which chapter do we read that good news from a distant land is like cool water to the soul? **25** (verse 25)

5. "The guilty flee when none pursue" is found in chapter: **28**

6. "The fear of the Lord is the beginning of ______..."
KNOWLEDGE (1:7) OR WISDOM (9:10)

7. "As _____ sharpens _____, so one man sharpens another": **IRON, IRON**

8. "Do not add to his words, or he will rebuke you and prove you a liar" is found in: **30:6.**

9. Which book follows Proverbs? **ECCLESIASTES**

10. Proverbs 13:24 reads, "He who spares the rod _____ his son." **HATES**

ANSWERS

Bible Quiz 46: Ecclesiastes

❶ To whom is this book attributed? ______________________________

❷ Ecclesiastes has 14 chapters: ❑ True or ❑ False?

❸ Which book follows Ecclesiastes in the Old Testament? ____________

❹ "There is a time for everything, and a season for every activity under heaven..." This famous poem is found in chapter __________________.

❺ "Whoever loves wealth is never satisfied with __________________" (5:10).

❻ "There is not a righteous man on earth who does what is right and never sins"—called "the Romans 3:23 of the Old Testament"—is found in __________________. ❑ 1:5 ❑ 4:4 ❑ 7:20 ❑ 12:14

❼ "If a man is _________________________, the rafters sag" (10:18).

❽ "Now all has been heard; here is the conclusion of the matter: Fear God and keep his commandments, for this is the whole duty of man. For God will bring every deed into judgment, including every hidden thing, whether it is good or evil." This passage appears in the middle chapter of Ecclesiastes: ❑ True or ❑ False?

❾ Who was the father of the Teacher? __________________________

❿ Life "under the sun" (without God) is _________________________.

Answers to Bible Quiz 46: Ecclesiastes

1. To whom is this book attributed? **SOLOMON**

2. Ecclesiastes has 14 chapters: **FALSE**. It has 12 chapters.

3. Which book follows Ecclesiastes in the Old Testament? **SONG OF SONGS**

4. "There is a time for everything, and a season for every activity under heaven…" This famous poem is found in chapter ____. **THREE**

5. "Whoever loves wealth is never satisfied with _____" (5:10). **HIS INCOME**

6. "There is not a righteous man on earth who does what is right and never sins"—called "the Romans 3:23 of the Old Testament"—is found in: **7:20**

7. "If a man is ____, the rafters sag" (10:18). **LAZY**

8. "Now all has been heard; here is the conclusion of the matter: Fear God and keep his commandments, for this is the whole duty of man. For God will bring every deed into judgment, including every hidden thing, whether it is good or evil." This passage appears in the middle chapter of Ecclesiastes: **FALSE**
It is the final passage of the book.

9. Who was the father of the Teacher? **DAVID**

10. Life "under the sun" (without God) is ______.
MEANINGLESS/EMPTY/VANITY/FUTILE

Bible Quiz 47: Song of Songs

1. Who does the groom appear to be in the Song? ________________

2. In which city is the Song set? ______________________________

3. (In some versions of the Song, at least) what is the name of the bride?

❑ Shunnamite ❑ Shulamith ❑ Shibboleth ❑ Shulammite

4. In chapter 2, we read the admonition, "Catch for us the ________..."

5. Which book of the Bible follows Song of Songs? ______________

6. Another name for this book is:

❑ Canticles ❑ Lovesick ❑ Ode to Love ❑ Lamentations

7. In Song 8:7a, we read "Many waters cannot __________; rivers cannot wash it away."

❑ stop romance ❑ quench love ❑ extinguish passion ❑ forgive sin

8. One refrain within the book is, "Do not arouse or awaken love until it so desires." A modern-day way of putting it might be:

❑ Let her sleep. ❑ True love waits. ❑ Obey your thirst. ❑ Love deeply.

9. The final passage of the book reads:

❑ "Come away, my lover, and be like a gazelle or like a young stag on the spice-laden mountains."

❑ "His left arm is under my head and his right arm embraces me."

❑ "His arms are rods of gold set with chrysolite. His body is like polished ivory decorated with sapphires."

❑ "I am a rose of Sharon, a lily of the valleys."

10. How many chapters does this book have? ❑ 4 ❑ 8 ❑ 12 ❑ 16

Answers to Bible Quiz 47: Song of Songs

1. Who does the groom appear to be in the Song? **SOLOMON**

2. In which city is the Song set? **JERUSALEM**

3. (In some versions of the Song, at least) what is the name of the bride? **SHULAMITH**—although Shulammite is also acceptable

4. In chapter 2, we read the admonition, "Catch for us the _____..." **FOXES OR JACKALS**

5. Which book of the Bible follows Song of Songs? **ISAIAH**

6. Another name for this book is: **CANTICLES**

7. In Song 8:7a, we read "Many waters cannot _____; rivers cannot wash it away." **QUENCH LOVE**

8. One refrain within the book is "Do not arouse or awaken love until it so desires." A modern-day way of putting it might be: **TRUE LOVE WAITS**

9. The final passage of the book reads: **"COME AWAY, MY LOVER, AND BE LIKE A GAZELLE OR LIKE A YOUNG STAG ON THE SPICE-LADEN MOUNTAINS."**

10. How many chapters does this book have? **8**

Bible Quiz 48: Isaiah

❶ During which century before Christ did Isaiah minister?

❑ 10th century B.C. (900s) ❑ 8th century B.C. (700s)

❑ 5th century B.C. (400s) ❑ 2nd century B.C. (100s)

❷ How many chapters are there in this relatively long book of the Bible?

❑ 44 ❑ 55 ❑ 66 ❑ 77 ❑ 88

❸ "Come now, let us reason together," appears in which chapter? ______

❹ What event in Isaiah's life takes place in chapter 6? _______________

❺ Who is the ultimate referent of the several "servant songs" (prophecies) in the book? ________________________________

❻ Which book precedes Isaiah? ___________________________

❼ Chapter 5 contains a parable. What is the subject? _______________

❑ The Prodigal Son ❑ The Vineyard

❑ The Lost Coins ❑ The Selfish Shepherd

❽ Isaiah warns the unrepentant of the certainty of exile, and at the same time offers hope that __________________ will take place afterwards.

❑ heaven ❑ showers of blessing

❑ return from captivity ❑ righteous sacrifices

❾ Which other prophet lived and prophesied at about the same time as Isaiah? ❑ Jeremiah ❑ Amos ❑ Elijah ❑ Habakkuk

❿ Which Gentile ruler is prophesied by name in chapter 44? _________

Answers to Bible Quiz 48: Isaiah

1. During which century before Christ did Isaiah minister? **8th century B.C. (700s)**

2. How many chapters are there in this relatively long book of the Bible? **66**

3. "Come now, let us reason together," appears in which chapter? **CHAPTER 1**

4. What event in Isaiah's life takes place in chapter 6? **HIS CALL TO BE A PROPHET**

5. Who is the ultimate referent of the several "servant songs" (prophecies) in the book? **JESUS CHRIST**

6. Which book precedes Isaiah? **SONG OF SONGS**

7. Chapter 5 contains a parable. What is the subject? **THE VINEYARD**

8. Isaiah warns the unrepentant of the certainty of exile, and at the same time offers hope that ____ will take place afterwards: **RETURN FROM CAPTIVITY**

9. Which other prophet lived and prophesied at about the same time as Isaiah? **AMOS**

10. Which Gentile ruler is prophesied by name in chapter 44? **CYRUS**

Bible Quiz 49: Jeremiah-Lamentations

❶ Jeremiah is the "before" and Lamentations is the "after":

❑ True or ❑ False?

❷ These books together have 57 chapters in all: ❑ True or ❑ False?

❸ What is the name of Jeremiah's "secretary," whose personal seal was identified just recently by archaeologists? ______________________

❹ Who actually cut slices off of Jeremiah's message and threw them into the fire (in chapter 36)? ❑ Saul ❑ Uzziah ❑ Jehoiakim ❑ David

❺ To which devastated and deserted city does Lamentations 1 refer?

____

❻ Do the words, "The steadfast love of the Lord never ceases…" (RSV) appear in Jeremiah or in Lamentations? ______________________

❼ The dates of Jeremiah's prophetic ministry are:

❑ 1010-970 B.C. ❑ 626-586 B.C. ❑ 433-393 B.C. ❑ 30 B.C.-11 A.D.

❽ The prophecy of the new covenant appears in Jeremiah chapter:

❑ 11 ❑ 31 ❑ 41 ❑ 61

❾ In chapter 20, Jeremiah curses the day of his birth: ❑ True or ❑ False?

❿ "The heart is deceitful…" appears in Jeremiah 19:7:

❑ True or ❑ False?

Answers to Bible Quiz 49: Jeremiah-Lamentations

1. Jeremiah is the "before" and Lamentations is the "after": **TRUE**

2. These books together have 57 chapters in all: **TRUE**

3. What is the name of Jeremiah's "secretary," whose personal seal was identified just recently by archaeologists? **BARUCH**

4. Who actually cut slices off of Jeremiah's message and threw them into the fire (in chapter 36)? **JEHOIAKIM**

5. To which devastated and deserted city does Lamentations 1 refer? **JERUSALEM**

6. Do the words, "The steadfast love of the Lord never ceases…" (RSV) appear in Jeremiah or in Lamentations? **LAMENTATIONS** (Chapter 3)

7. The dates of Jeremiah's prophetic ministry are: **626-586 B.C.**

8. The prophecy of the new covenant appears in Jeremiah chapter: **31**

9. In chapter 20, Jeremiah curses the day of his birth: **TRUE**

10. "The heart is deceitful…" appears in Jeremiah 19:7: **FALSE.** The passage is 17:9.

Bible Quiz 50: Ezekiel

❶ Which book of the Bible comes right before Ezekiel?

____

❷ The passage about the Good Shepherd appears in chapter:

❑ 24 ❑ 34 ❑ 44 ❑ 54

❸ Ezekiel lived in: ❑ 900s B.C. ❑ 500s B.C. ❑ 300s B.C. ❑ 100s B.C.

❹ Gog and Magog, unspecified enemies of the people of God, are mentioned in the book of Ezekiel: ❑ True or ❑ False?

❺ The Vision of the Dry Bones appears in Ezekiel 37:

❑ True or ❑ False?

❻ The Allegory of Unfaithful Jerusalem appears in Ezekiel 16:

❑ True or ❑ False?

❼ Chapters 3 and 33 both contain passages about the watchman. Which musical instrument was the watchman supposed to sound to alert the people of the approaching enemy? ______________________

❽ Which book immediately follows Ezekiel? ______________________

❾ Which figure is mentioned in the closing chapters of the book?

❑ The Antichrist ❑ The Hatchet Man ❑ The Prince ❑ The Princess

❿ Evil practices denounced in Ezekiel include all the following except:

❑ idolatry ❑ heliolatry (sun worship) ❑ sacrificing to the Queen of Heaven ❑ whitewashing their sin

Answers to Bible Quiz 50: Ezekiel

1. Which book of the Bible comes right before Ezekiel? **LAMENTATIONS**

2. The passage about the Good Shepherd appears in chapter: **34**

3. Ezekiel lived in: **500s B.C.**

4. Gog and Magog, unspecified enemies of the people of God, are mentioned in the book of Ezekiel: **TRUE**

5. The Vision of the Dry Bones appears in Ezekiel 37: **TRUE**

6. The Allegory of Unfaithful Jerusalem appears in Ezekiel 16: **TRUE**

7. Chapters 3 and 33 both contain passages about the watchman. Which musical instrument was the watchman supposed to sound to alert the people of the approaching enemy? **TRUMPET**

8. Which book immediately follows Ezekiel? **DANIEL**

9. Which figure is mentioned in the closing chapters of the book? **THE PRINCE**

10. Evil practices denounced in Ezekiel include all the following except: **SACRIFICING TO THE QUEEN OF HEAVEN**

ANSWERS

Bible Quiz 51: Daniel

❶ The Ancient of Days is mentioned in Daniel chapter:

❑ 1 ❑ 2 ❑ 7 ❑ 12

❷ The Resurrection is mentioned in Daniel chapter: ❑ 1 ❑ 2 ❑ 7 ❑ 12

❸ The dream of Nebuchadnezzar is explained in Daniel chapter:

❑ 1 ❑ 2 ❑ 7 ❑ 12

❹ Daniel refuses to eat contaminated Gentile food in Daniel chapter:

❑ 1 ❑ 2 ❑ 7 ❑ 12

❺ How many chapters are there in Daniel? ____________________

❻ Which languages is the book written in? ____________________

❼ Which biblical book follows Daniel? ____________________

❽ Daniel was thrown into a blazing furnace: ❑ True or ❑ False?

❾ Daniel was thrown into the lions' den: ❑ True or ❑ False?

❿ What was written on the wall before Belshazzar's eyes (chapter 5)?

❑ Eloi Eloi Lama Sabachthani

❑ Talitha Koum Marana Tha

❑ Mene Mene Tekel Parsin

❑ Maher Shalal Hash Baz

Answers to Bible Quiz 51: Daniel

1. The Ancient of Days is mentioned in Daniel chapter: **7**
2. The Resurrection is mentioned in Daniel chapter: **12**
3. The dream of Nebuchadnezzar is explained in Daniel chapter: **2**
4. Daniel refuses to eat contaminated Gentile food in Daniel chapter: **1**
5. How many chapters are there in Daniel? **TWELVE**
6. Which languages is the book written in? **HEBREW AND ARAMAIC**
7. Which biblical book follows Daniel? **HOSEA**
8. Daniel was thrown into a blazing furnace: **FALSE**
9. Daniel was thrown into the lions' den: **TRUE**
10. What was written on the wall before Belshazzar's eyes (chapter 5)?

MENE MENE TEKEL PARSIN

ANSWERS

Bible Quiz 52: Hosea

❶ What is the parallel developed in this book between Hosea's life and the spiritual life of Israel? ________________________________

❷ Who (presumably) wrote Hosea? ________________________

❸ Who was Hosea's unfaithful wife? ______________________

❹ How many chapters are there in this book? ❑ 8 ❑ 14 ❑ 20 ❑ 22

❺ Which book follows Hosea? ____________________________

❻ Hosea prophesied during the reigns of Uzziah, Jotham, Ahaz and Hezekiah in the 6th century B.C.: ❑ True or ❑ False?

❼ Who were Jezreel, Lo-Ruhamah and Lo-Ammi? _______________

❽ Hosea 6:6, "For I desire mercy, not sacrifice, and acknowledgment of God rather than burnt offerings," is quoted twice in the book of Matthew. By whom is it quoted? ____________________________________

❾ Hoshea is another form of Yeshua (Jesus' name). What is the meaning of Hoshea? ____

❿ Hosea is the first of the Minor Prophets. How many more are there?

____

Answers to Bible Quiz 52: Hosea

1. What is the parallel developed in this book between Hosea's life and the spiritual life of Israel? **ADULTERY** (Marital and Spiritual/National)

2. Who (presumably) wrote Hosea? **HOSEA**

3. Who was Hosea's unfaithful wife? **GOMER**

4. How many chapters are there in this book? **14**

5. Which book follows Hosea? **JOEL**

6. Hosea prophesied during the reigns of Uzziah, Jotham, Ahaz and Hezekiah in the 6th century B.C.: **FALSE.** Right Kings, wrong century (try the eighth century B.C.).

7. Who were Jezreel, Lo-Ruhamah and Lo-Ammi?
CHILDREN OF HOSEA AND GOMER

8. Hosea 6:6, "For I desire mercy, not sacrifice, and acknowledgment of God rather than burnt offerings," is quoted twice in the book of Matthew. By whom is it quoted? **JESUS**

9. Hoshea is another form of Yeshua (Jesus' name). What is the meaning of Hoshea? **SALVATION**

10. Hosea is the first of the Minor Prophets. How many more are there? **ELEVEN**

ANSWERS

Bible Quiz 53: Joel

❶ Joel compares the invading foreign army to:

❑ spiders ❑ ants ❑ locusts ❑ scorpions

❷ The 6th-century invader is Babylon: ❑ True or ❑ False?

❸ How many chapters are there in Joel? ____________________

❹ Which other books of the Minor Prophets have this same number of chapters? ____

❺ Peter quotes from Joel 2 in Acts chapter ___________________.

❻ Joel was the son of Pethuel: ❑ True or ❑ False?

❼ Joel 3:10, reversing Isaiah 2:4, reads "Beat your plowshares into swords and your pruning hooks into ___________________. Let the weakling say, 'I am strong!'"

❽ "Multitudes, multitudes in the valley of ______________" (Joel 3:14):

❑ the Shadow of Death ❑ the Dolls ❑ Decision ❑ the Dinosaurs

❾ The book before Joel is: ________________________________.

❿ "A nation has invaded my land, powerful and without number; it has the teeth of a lion, the fangs of a _________________________" (1:6).

Answers to Bible Quiz 53: Joel

1. Joel compares the invading foreign army to: **LOCUSTS**

2. The 6th-century invader is Babylon: **TRUE**

3. How many chapters are there in Joel? **THREE**

4. Which other books of the Minor Prophets have this same number of chapters?

NAHUM, HABAKKUK AND ZEPHANIAH

5. Peter quotes from Joel 2 in Acts chapter _____. **TWO**

6. Joel was the son of Pethuel: **TRUE**

7. Joel 3:10, reversing Isaiah 2:4, reads "Beat your plowshares into swords and your pruning hooks into _____. Let the weakling say, 'I am strong!'"

SPEARS

8. "Multitudes, multitudes in the valley of _____" (Joel 3:14) **DECISION**

9. The book before Joel is _____. **HOSEA**

10. "A nation has invaded my land, powerful and without number; it has the teeth of a lion, the fangs of a _____" (1:6). **LIONESS**

Bible Quiz 54: Amos

❶ ❷ What were Amos' two professions before becoming a prophet?

____

❸ The king of Judah when Amos prophesied was Uzziah. The king of Israel was: ❑ Jeroboam II ❑ Solomon ❑ Zedekiah ❑ Ahab

❹ ❺ The crescendo of judgment in chapters 1-2 begins with prophecies against Damascus, Gaza, Tyre, Edom, Ammon and Moab. Who are the final two nations named in the list? ________________________

❻ Amos has 11 chapters: ❑ True or ❑ False?

❼ Amos 5:21 reads, "I hate, I despise your religious feasts; I cannot stand your ____."

❽ The famous Amos 5:24 reads, "But let ________________roll on like a river, righteousness like a never-failing stream!"

❾ What is the book following Amos—and the subject of the next quiz?

____

❿ The encouraging words of 9:13 are, "'The days are coming,' declares the LORD, 'when the _________________ will be overtaken by the plowman and the planter by the one treading grapes.'"

Answers to Bible Quiz 54: Amos

1-2. What were Amos' two professions before becoming a prophet?

SHEPHERD AND DRESSER OF SYCAMORE-FIG TREES (7:14)

3. The king of Judah when Amos prophesied was Uzziah. The king of Israel was:

JEROBOAM II (son of Jehoash)

4-5. The crescendo of judgment in chapters 1-2 begins with prophecies against Damascus, Gaza, Tyre, Edom, Ammon and Moab. Who are the final two nations named in the list?

JUDAH AND ISRAEL (respectively)

6. Amos has 11 chapters: **FALSE.** It has nine.

7. Amos 5:21 reads, "I hate, I despise your religious feasts; I cannot stand your _____." **RELIGIOUS ASSEMBLIES**

8. The famous Amos 5:24 reads, "But let _____ roll on like a river, righteousness like a never-failing stream!" **JUSTICE**

9. What is the book following Amos—and the subject of the next quiz?

OBADIAH

10. The encouraging words of 9:13 are: "'The days are coming,' declares the LORD, 'when the _____ will be overtaken by the plowman and the planter by the one treading grapes.'" **REAPER**

ANSWERS

Bible Quiz 55: Obadiah

❶ How many chapters are there in this book of the Bible? ___________

❷ How many other books in the Bible have the same (surprising) number of chapters? ____

❸ Obadiah means "servant of Yah[weh]": ❑ True or ❑ False?

❹ According to 1:1, the oracle is about/against which nation? Hint: 1:6 reads, "But how Esau will be ransacked, his hidden treasures pillaged!"

____

❺ Lamenting the deplorable behavior of this same nation on the day Babylon destroyed Zion, the Lord said through Obadiah, "On the day you stood aloof while strangers carried off his wealth and foreigners entered his gates and cast lots for Jerusalem, you were ________________."

❻ Which book follows Obadiah? ________________________

❼ Which book precedes Obadiah? ________________________

❽ The theme of Obadiah may be said to be:

❑ enemies versus friends ❑ holiness versus ungodliness

❑ revenge versus forgiveness ❑ looking down versus looking up

❾ This book is quoted twice in the New Testament: ❑ True or ❑ False?

❿ The final verse of the book is, "Deliverers will go up on Mount Zion to govern the mountains of Esau. And the kingdom will be

________________________."

Answers to Bible Quiz 55: Obadiah

1. How many chapters are there in this book of the Bible? **ONE**

2. How many other books in the Bible have the same (surprising) number of chapters? **FOUR** (Philemon, 2 John, 3 John, Jude)

3. Obadiah means "servant of Yah[weh]": **TRUE**

4. According to 1:1, the oracle is about/against which nation? Hint: 1:6 reads, "But how Esau will be ransacked, his hidden treasures pillaged!" **EDOM**

5. Lamenting the deplorable behavior of this same nation on the day Babylon destroyed Zion, the Lord said through Obadiah, "On the day you stood aloof while strangers carried off his wealth and foreigners entered his gates and cast lots for Jerusalem, you were_____." **LIKE ONE OF THEM**

6. Which book follows Obadiah? **JONAH**

7. Which book precedes Obadiah? **AMOS**

8. The theme of Obadiah may be said to be: **REVENGE VERSUS FORGIVENESS**

9. This book is quoted twice in the New Testament: True or False? **FALSE**

10. The final verse of the book is "Deliverers will go up on Mount Zion to govern the mountains of Esau. And the kingdom will be _____." **THE LORD'S**

Bible Quiz 56: Jonah

❶ To which nation was Jonah sent to preach?

❑ Assyria ❑ Babylon ❑ Persia ❑ Greece

❷ How many chapters are there in this short book? ________________

❸ What did Jonah do upon boarding the ship bound for Tarshish?

____

❹ What did the sailors do to Jonah after his repeated insistence that they do so? ____

❺ What did Jonah do while in the interior of the large animal that swallowed him? ____

❻ What was the reason he fled from the mission on which the Lord had sent him? ____

❼ The prophecy of warning stated that Nineveh would be destroyed in ________________________ days.

❽ The king of Nineveh failed to repent: ❑ True or ❑ False?

❾ Jonah wanted the Ninevites to be destroyed: ❑ True or ❑ False?

❿ What was apparently the population of the city?

❑ 1,200 ❑ 12,000 ❑120,000 ❑ 1,200,000

Answers to Bible Quiz 56: Jonah

1. To which nation was Jonah sent to preach? **ASSYRIA**

2. How many chapters are there in this short book? **FOUR**

3. What did Jonah do upon boarding the ship bound for Tarshish? **FELL ASLEEP**

4. What did the sailors do to Jonah after his repeated insistence that they do so? **THREW HIM OVERBOARD**

5. What did Jonah do while in the interior of the large animal that swallowed him? **PRAYED**

6. What was the reason he fled from the mission on which the Lord had sent him? **PREJUDICE.** He did not want to share God with the Gentiles.

7. The prophecy of warning stated that Nineveh would be destroyed in ___ days. **40**

8. The king of Nineveh failed to repent: **FALSE**

9. Jonah wanted the Ninevites to be destroyed: **TRUE**

10. What was apparently the population of the city? **120,000**

Bible Quiz 57: Micah

❶ Micah spoke in the 600s B.C., shortly before the invasion of the Babylonians: ❑ True or ❑ False?

❷ In which chapter is the birthplace of the Messiah prophesied? _______

❸ Micah engages the service of an idolatrous priest in the book of Judges: ❑ True or ❑ False?

❹ Micah prophesied concerning Samaria and __________ (Micah 1:1).

❺ The most famous passage in all of Micah may be 6:8. It reads, "He has showed you, O man, what is good. And what does the LORD require of you? To act justly and to love mercy and to ________ with your God."
❑ walk humbly ❑ commune in silence ❑ compromise commitment
❑ speak reverently

❻ Which book follows Micah in the Bible? ____________________

❼ The prophecy of 4:1, whose fulfillment takes place in the church of Christ, reads: "In the last days the mountain of the LORD's temple will be established as chief among the mountains; it will be raised above the hills, and _______________." ❑ the other mountains will be flattened
❑ peoples will stream to it ❑ great will be the power of the Almighty
❑ yea, even the hillbillies shall come thereto

❽ How many chapters does Micah have? ❑ 1 ❑ 3 ❑ 5 ❑ 7 ❑ 9

❾ Jeremiah 26:18 says Micah of Moresheth prophesied in the days of:
❑ Hezekiah ❑ Saul ❑ Zedekiah ❑ Manasseh

❿ In 1:4, what happens when the Lord comes down from his dwelling places and treads the high places of the earth? ❑ The mountains melt
❑ The valleys split apart ❑ Neither A nor B ❑ Both A and B

Answers to Bible Quiz 57: Micah

1. Micah spoke in the 600s B.C., shortly before the invasion of the Babylonians: **FALSE. MICAH MINISTERED MANY YEARS BEFORE THE BABYLONIAN INVASION**

2. In which chapter is the birthplace of the Messiah prophesied? **FIVE**

3. Micah engages the service of an idolatrous priest in the book of Judges: **TRUE.** But this is a different Micah.

4. Micah prophesied concerning Samaria and ______ (Micah 1:1). **JERUSALEM**

5. The most famous passage in all of Micah may be 6:8. It reads, "He has showed you, O man, what is good. And what does the LORD require of you? To act justly and to love mercy and to _____ with your God." **WALK HUMBLY**

6. Which book follows Micah in the Bible? **NAHUM**

7. The prophecy of 4:1, whose fulfillment takes place in the church of Christ, reads: "In the last days the mountain of the LORD's temple will be established as chief among the mountains; it will be raised above the hills, and _____." **PEOPLES WILL STREAM TO IT**

8. How many chapters does Micah have? **7**

9. Jeremiah 26:18 says Micah of Moresheth prophesied in the days of: **HEZEKIAH**

10. In 1:4, what happens when the Lord comes down from his dwelling places and treads the high places of the earth? Both A & B, **THE MOUNTAINS MELT AND THE VALLEYS SPLIT APART**

Bible Quiz 58: Nahum and Habakkuk

❶ Nahum prophesied concerning:

❑ Nineveh ❑ Nimrud ❑ Nanjing ❑ Nantucket

❷ Habakkuk prophesied concerning: ❑ Judah ❑ Israel ❑ Egypt ❑ Moab

❸ Nahum has three chapters: ❑ True or ❑ False?

❹ Habakkuk has three chapters: ❑ True or ❑ False?

❺ "Nothing can heal your wound; your injury is fatal. Everyone who hears the news about you claps his hands at your fall, for who has not felt your endless cruelty?" Are these words the final verse of Nahum or Habakkuk? ______________________________

❻ "Though the fig tree does not bud and there are no grapes on the vines, though the olive crop fails and the fields produce no food, though there are no sheep in the pen and no cattle in the stalls, yet I will rejoice in the LORD, I will be joyful in God my Savior. The Sovereign LORD is my strength; he makes my feet like the feet of a deer, he enables me to go on the heights…" Are these words the final verses of Nahum or Habakkuk?

____

❼ Which book precedes Nahum? ______________________________

❽ Which book follows Habakkuk? ______________________________

❾ Which prophet questions God about his justice? ____________________

❿ Which prophet does Paul quote in Romans when he writes, "He who by faith is righteous shall live," or, "The righteous will live by faith"?

____

Answers to Bible Quiz 58: Nahum and Habakkuk

1. Nahum prophesied concerning: **NINEVEH**

2. Habakkuk prophesied concerning: **JUDAH**

3. Nahum has three chapters: **TRUE**

4. Habakkuk has three chapters: **TRUE**

5. "Nothing can heal your wound; your injury is fatal. Everyone who hears the news about you claps his hands at your fall, for who has not felt your endless cruelty?" Are these words the final verse of Nahum or Habakkuk?: **NAHUM**

6. "Though the fig tree does not bud and there are no grapes on the vines, though the olive crop fails and the fields produce no food, though there are no sheep in the pen and no cattle in the stalls, yet I will rejoice in the LORD, I will be joyful in God my Savior. The Sovereign LORD is my strength; he makes my feet like the feet of a deer, he enables me to go on the heights…" Are these words the final verses of Nahum or Habakkuk?: **HABAKKUK**

7. Which book precedes Nahum? **MICAH**

8. Which book follows Habakkuk? **ZEPHANIAH**

9. Which prophet questions God about his justice? **HABAKKUK**

10. Which prophet does Paul quote in Romans when he writes, "He who by faith is righteous shall live," or, "The righteous will live by faith"? **HABAKKUK**

Bible Quiz 59: Zephaniah and Haggai

❶ Which of these two books is longer? ______________________

❷ How many chapters does the shorter of the two contain? _________

❸ The longer one contains fourteen chapters: ❑ True or ❑ False?

❹ Zephaniah's message came during the time of King Josiah.

Approximately when was that?

❑ 780-770 B.C. ❑ 710-700 B.C. ❑ 660-650 B.C. ❑ 620-610 B.C.

❺ Haggai's message came in the time of King Darius of Persia.

Approximately when was that?

❑ 700-690 B.C. ❑ 600-590 B.C. ❑ 520-510 B.C. ❑ 440-430 B.C.

❻ Who was Haggai's fellow prophet who challenged the Jews to rebuild the Temple? ______________________________________

❼ The challenge to rebuild the Temple came after the time of Nehemiah:

❑ True or ❑ False?

❽ Which book follows Haggai? ____________________________

❾ Zephaniah 1:5 refers to the worship of Baal and Molech by Judah:

❑ True or ❑ False?

❿ Which prophet said, "Is it a time for you yourselves to be living in your paneled houses, while this house remains a ruin?"

____

Answers to Bible Quiz 59: Zephaniah and Haggai

1. Which of these two books is longer? **ZEPHANIAH**

2. How many chapters does the shorter of the two contain? **TWO**

3. The longer one contains 14 chapters: **FALSE.** It has only three.

4. Zephaniah's message came during the time of King Josiah. Approximately when was that? **620-610 B.C.**

5. Haggai's message came in the time of King Darius of Persia. Approximately when was that? **520-510 B.C.**

6. Who was Haggai's fellow prophet who challenged the Jews to rebuild the Temple? **ZECHARIAH**

7. This was after the time of Nehemiah: **FALSE**

8. Which book follows Haggai? **ZECHARIAH**

9. Zephaniah 1:5 refers to the worship of Baal and Molech by Judah: **TRUE**

10. Which prophet said, "Is it a time for you yourselves to be living in your paneled houses, while this house remains a ruin?" **HAGGAI** (1:4)

Bible Quiz 60: Zechariah and Malachi

❶ Malachi is the last book of the English Bible: ❑ True or ❑ False?

❷ Malachi is the last book of the Hebrew Bible: ❑ True or ❑ False?

❸ Malachi wrote in the 400s B.C.: ❑ True or ❑ False?

❹ Zechariah wrote in the 500s B.C.: ❑ True or ❑ False?

❺ Who was Zechariah's partner in preaching and prophecy, motivating the people of God to rebuild the Temple? ________________________

❻ Which book foretells the coming of John the Baptist?

____

❼ In which book does God say, "I hate divorce"? __________________

❽ Which book contains more Messianic prophecy (by far)?

____

❾ How many books of the Bible start with the letter "Z"

____

❿ Which book of the Bible is Zechariah?

❑ 38th ❑ 40th ❑ 43rd ❑ 45th

Answers to Bible Quiz 60: Zechariah and Malachi

1. Malachi is the last book of the English Bible: **FALSE.**

Revelation is the last book.

2. Malachi is the last book of the Hebrew Bible: **FALSE.** It is Chronicles.

3. Malachi wrote in the 400s B.C.: **TRUE**

4. Zechariah wrote in the 500s B.C.: **TRUE**

5. Who was Zechariah's partner in preaching and prophecy, motivating the people of God to rebuild the Temple? **HAGGAI**

6. Which book foretells the coming of John the Baptist? **MALACHI**

7. In which book does God say, "I hate divorce"? **MALACHI**

8. Which book contains more Messianic prophecy (by far)? **ZECHARIAH**

9. How many books of the Bible start with the letter "Z"? **TWO**

10. Which book of the Bible is Zechariah? **38TH**

Bible Quiz 61: The Gospel of Matthew

❶ The Sermon on the Mount is found in Matthew: ❑ True or ❑ False?

❷ The Great Commission is found in Matthew: ❑ True or ❑ False?

❸ The Greatest Commandment is found in Matthew and Mark, but not in Luke: ❑ True or ❑ False?

❹ The Golden Rule is found in Matthew: ❑ True or ❑ False?

❺ Matthew begins with: ❑ genealogy ❑ Jesus' baptism ❑ the Resurrection ❑ the sermon in Nazareth

❻ Matthew has 28 chapters: ❑ True or ❑ False?

❼ Matthew's conversion is found in Matthew:

❑ 9:9 ❑ 10:10 ❑ 11:11 ❑ 12:12

❽ The book immediately before Matthew is Malachi:

❑ True or ❑ False?

❾ The Parable of the Sheep and the Goats does not appear in Matthew:

❑ True or ❑ False?

❿ The chapter of Matthew that is rich in parables is chapter:

❑ 13 ❑ 14 ❑ 15 ❑ 16

Answers to Bible Quiz 61: The Gospel of Matthew

1. The Sermon on the Mount is found in Matthew: **TRUE**

2. The Great Commission is found in Matthew: **TRUE**

3. The Greatest Commandment is found in Matthew and Mark, but not in Luke: **FALSE.** It is found in all three.

4. The Golden Rule is found in Matthew: **TRUE**

5. Matthew begins with: **GENEALOGY**

6. Matthew has 28 chapters: **TRUE**

7. Matthew's conversion is found in Matthew: **9:9**

8. The book immediately before Matthew is Malachi: **TRUE**

9. The Parable of the Sheep and the Goats does not appear in Matthew: **FALSE**

10. The chapter of Matthew that is rich in parables is chapter: **13**

Bible Quiz 62: The Gospel of Mark

❶ Mark is the shortest of the four gospels: ❑ True or ❑ False?

❷ The crucifixion is recounted in Mark chapter 15: ❑ True or ❑ False?

❸ The ending of Mark's gospel is uncertain: ❑ True or ❑ False?

❹ "Very early in the morning, while it was still dark, Jesus got up, left the house and went off to a solitary place, where he ____________________" (Mark 1:35).

❺ Mark's gospel begins, "In the beginning was the Word":

❑ True or ❑ False?

❻ Jesus predicts the Roman destruction of Jerusalem in chapter 13:

❑ True or ❑ False?

❼ Mark is the 41st book of the Bible: ❑ True or ❑ False?

❽ 'Then he called the crowd to him along with his disciples and said: "If anyone would come after me, he must deny himself and take up his cross and follow me." This verse appears in chapter:

❑ 8 ❑ 13 ❑ 16 ❑ none of the preceding

❾ The dance of Herodias' daughter, which led to John the Baptist's decapitation, is recounted in Mark, Matthew and Luke: ❑ True or ❑ False?

❿ The Gerasene Demoniac is exorcised in chapter 5: ❑ True or ❑ False?

Answers to Bible Quiz 62: The Gospel of Mark

1. Mark is the shortest of the four gospels: **TRUE**

2. The Crucifixion is recounted in Mark chapter 15: **TRUE**

3. The ending of Mark's gospel is uncertain: **TRUE**

4. "Very early in the morning, while it was still dark, Jesus got up, left the house and went off to a solitary place, where he ____" (Mark 1:35). **PRAYED**

5. Mark's gospel begins, "In the beginning was the Word": **FALSE**

6. Jesus predicts the Roman destruction of Jerusalem in chapter 13: **TRUE**

7. Mark is the 41st book of the Bible: **TRUE**

8. "Then he called the crowd to him along with his disciples and said: 'If anyone would come after me, he must deny himself and take up his cross and follow me.'" This verse appears in chapter: **8**

9. The dance of Herodias' daughter, which led to John the Baptist's decapitation, is recounted in Mark, Matthew and Luke: **FALSE.** It does not appear in Luke.

10. The Gerasene Demoniac is exorcised in chapter 5: **TRUE**

Bible Quiz 63: The Gospel of Luke

❶ In pure length, Luke is the longest of the four gospels:

❑ True or ❑ False?

❷ The sequel to Luke is ________________________________.

❸ What was Luke's profession? ____________________________

❹ The Emmaus Road incident appears only in Luke: ❑ True or ❑ False?

❺ Which book immediately follows Luke? ____________________

❻ Who was the high priest and son-in-law of Annas? ______________

❼ The Resurrection occurs in Luke chapter: ❑ 21 ❑ 22 ❑ 23 ❑ 24

❽ The Sermon on the Plain is found in Luke 6: ❑ True or ❑ False?

❾ In Luke 13, Jesus calls Herod Antipas a "____________________."

❿ The thief on the cross is pardoned only in Luke's gospel:

❑ True or ❑ False?

Answers to Bible Quiz 63: The Gospel of Luke

1. In pure length, Luke is the longest of the four gospels: **TRUE**
2. The sequel to Luke is _____. **ACTS**
3. What was Luke's profession? **PHYSICIAN** (Colossians 4:14)
4. The Emmaus Road incident appears only in Luke: **TRUE**
5. Which book immediately follows Luke? **JOHN**
6. Who was the high priest and son-in-law of Annas? **CAIAPHAS**
7. The Resurrection occurs in Luke: **24**
8. The Sermon on the Plain is found in Luke 6: **TRUE**
9. In Luke 13, Jesus calls Herod Antipas a "_____." **FOX**
10. The thief on the cross is pardoned only in Luke's gospel: **TRUE**

ANSWERS

Bible Quiz 64: The Gospel of John

❶ Within this gospel, the "disciple whom Jesus loved" is apparently

____.

❷ John has 21 chapters: ❑ True or ❑ False?

❸ Jesus turned water to wine at: ❑ Shechem in Samaria

❑ Cana in Galilee ❑ Jerusalem in Benjamin ❑ Damascus in Syria

❹ Jesus washes the disciples' feet in John 12: ❑ True or ❑ False?

❺ The Crucifixion is recounted in chapter 19: ❑ True or ❑ False?

❻ Who was raised from the dead in John 11? ____________________

❼ Name his two sisters. ________________________________

❽ The "high priestly prayer" is found in chapter: ❑ 14 ❑ 17 ❑ 20 ❑ 24

❾ Nicodemus is only mentioned in John's gospel: ❑ True or ❑ False?

❿ "Jesus did many other things as well. If every one of them were written down, I suppose that even the whole world would not have room for the books that would be written." This is the last verse of John:

❑ True or ❑ False?

Answers to Bible Quiz 64: The Gospel of John

1. Within this gospel, the "disciple whom Jesus loved" is apparently _____.

JOHN

2. John has 21 chapters: **TRUE**

3. Jesus turned water to wine at: **CANA IN GALILEE**

4. Jesus washes the disciples' feet in John 12: **FALSE.** It was in chapter 13.

5. The Crucifixion is recounted in chapter 19: **TRUE**

6. Who was raised from the dead in John 11? **LAZARUS**

7. Name his two sisters. **MARY AND MARTHA**

8. The "high priestly prayer" is found in chapter: **17**

9. Nicodemus is only mentioned in John's gospel: **TRUE**

10. "Jesus did many other things as well. If every one of them were written down, I suppose that even the whole world would not have room for the books that would be written." This is the last verse of John: **TRUE**

Bible Quiz 65: Acts

❶ Which book of the Bible is Acts?

❑ The 5th ❑ The 43rd ❑ The 44th ❑ The 52nd

❷ Acts covers only one generation of church history: ❑ True or ❑ False?

❸ The book of Acts ends with Paul's execution during the reign of Nero:

❑ True or ❑ False?

❹ Peter's execution was scheduled to take place in Acts 12:

❑ True or ❑ False?

❺ James' execution took place in Acts 14: ❑ True or ❑ False?

❻ Who was Paul's traveling companion in Acts?

❑ Levi ❑ Luke ❑ Clement ❑ Elmo

❼ In chapter 15, a council convened to discuss the radical view that Gentiles must become Jews before they become Christians. In which city did this council take place? ______________________________

❽ Whom did Paul circumcise in chapter 16? ____________________

❾ In which city is the Areopagus, where Paul preached in chapter 17?

____

❿ In the New Testament, what book comes after Acts? ______________

Answers to Bible Quiz 65: Acts

1. Which book of the Bible is Acts? **THE 44TH**

2. Acts covers only one generation of church history: **TRUE**

3. The book of Acts ends with Paul's execution during the reign of Nero: **FALSE**

4. Peter's execution was scheduled to take place in Acts 12: **TRUE**

5. James' execution took place in Acts 14: **FALSE**

6. Who was Paul's traveling companion in Acts? **LUKE**

7. In chapter 15, a council convened to discuss the radical view that Gentiles must become Jews before they become Christians. In which city did this council take place? **JERUSALEM**

8. Whom did Paul circumcise in chapter 16? **TIMOTHY**

9. In which city is the Areopagus, where Paul preached in chapter 17? **ATHENS**

10. In the New Testament, what book comes after Acts? **ROMANS**

Bible Quiz 66: Romans

❶ This famous epistle was written to disciples in which city?

____

❷ Had the writer visited the city previously? ____________________

❸ Who was the writer? ____________________________________

❹ The theme of the book is found in:

❑ 1:17 ❑ 2:12 ❑ 3:23 ❑ 14:1.

❺ How many chapters does Romans have? ______________________

❻ The letter comes immediately between Acts and 1 Corinthians:

❑ True or ❑ False?

❼ Chapters 9-11 are concerned with the salvation of:

❑ Israel ❑ Gentiles ❑ Samaritans ❑ all three groups

❽ Some people think Romans 4 (justified by faith) directly contradicts

James chapter ____________ (justified by works). ❑ 1 ❑ 2 ❑ 3 ❑ 4

❾ Baptism is described as death, burial and resurrection with Christ in

chapter: ❑ 5 ❑ 6 ❑ 8 ❑ 13

❿ Romans 14 discusses judgment: ❑ True or ❑ False?

Answers to Bible Quiz 66: Romans

1. This famous epistle was written to disciples in which city? **ROME**
2. Had the writer visited the city previously? **NO**
3. Who was the writer? **PAUL**
4. The theme of the book is found in: **1:17**
5. How many chapters does Romans have? **16**
6. The letter comes immediately between Acts and 1 Corinthians: **TRUE**
7. Chapters 9-11 are concerned with the salvation of: **ISRAEL**
8. Some people think Romans 4 (justified by faith) directly contradicts James chapter ____ (justified by works): **2**
9. Baptism is described as death, burial and resurrection with Christ in chapter: **6**
10. Romans 14 discusses judgment: **TRUE**

ANSWERS

Bible Quiz 67: 1 and 2 Corinthians

❶ In which Corinthian chapter do we find the famous Ode to Love?

____

❷ In which Corinthian chapter does Paul tell us that he was under such pressure in Asia that he felt the sentence of death? __________________

❸ How many chapters are there in these two letters combined?

❑ 21 ❑ 25 ❑ 29 ❑ 33

❹ Where was Corinth located? ❑ Italy ❑ Greece ❑ Syria ❑ Cyprus

❺ The extended discussion of the Lord's Supper is found in 1 Corinthians chapter ____.

❻ The extended discussion of the relief offering for poor Christians is found in 2 Corinthians chapters ____________________________.

❼ Which book comes after 2 Corinthians? ______________________

❽ In 1 Corinthians 12, Paul mentions his "thorn in the flesh":

❑ True or ❑ False?

❾ In 2 Corinthians 7, Paul says that singles with the gift of celibacy ought to remain unmarried: ❑ True or ❑ False?

❿ Paul established the Corinthian church in Acts 10: ❑ True or ❑ False?

Answers to Bible Quiz 67: 1 and 2 Corinthians

1. In which Corinthian chapter do we find the famous Ode to Love?

1 CORINTHIANS 13

2. In which Corinthian chapter does Paul tell us that he was under such pressure in Asia that he felt the sentence of death? **2 CORINTHIANS 1**

3. How many chapters are there in these two letters combined? **TWENTY-NINE** (16+13)

4. Where was Corinth located? **GREECE**

5. The extended discussion of the Lord's Supper is found in 1 Corinthians chapter ______. **11**

6. The extended discussion of the relief offering for poor Christians is found in 2 Corinthians chapters ______. **8-9**

7. Which book comes after 2 Corinthians? **GALATIANS**

8. In 1 Corinthians 12, Paul mentions his "thorn in the flesh": **FALSE.** It is found in 2 Corinthians 12.

9. In 2 Corinthians 7, Paul says that singles with the gift of celibacy ought to remain unmarried: **FALSE.** That is found in 1 Corinthians 7.

10. Paul established the Corinthian church in Acts 10: **FALSE.** Acts 18 is the correct chapter.

ANSWERS

Bible Quiz 68: Galatians and Ephesians

❶ Who wrote these two letters? ______________________________

❷ Each has the same number of chapters. How many? _____________

❸ The image of the church as the bride of Christ is found in Galatians: ❑ True or ❑ False?

❹ The statement, "He gave some to be apostles, some to be prophets…" is found in Ephesians: ❑ True or ❑ False?

❺ The famous passage about the full armor (panoply) of God is found in Galatians: ❑ True or ❑ False?

❻ The passage, "I am astonished that you are so quickly abandoning the one who called you…" is found in Ephesians 1: ❑ True or ❑ False?

❼ The yoke of slavery to the law is mentioned in Galatians 5: ❑ True or ❑ False?

❽ "Awake, O sleeper! Rise from the dead, and Christ will shine on you," is thought by most scholars to be a baptismal hymn. It is found in Ephesians 5: ❑ True or ❑ False?

❾ Which book follows Ephesians? ___________________________

❿ The declaration, "From now on let no one cause me trouble, for I bear the marks [stigmata] of Jesus on my body," is found at the end of Galatians: ❑ True or ❑ False?

Answers to Bible Quiz 68: Galatians and Ephesians

1. Who wrote these two letters? **PAUL**

2. Each has the same number of chapters. How many? **SIX**

3. The image of the church as the bride of Christ is found in Galatians: **FALSE.** It is found in Ephesians 5.

4. The statement, "He gave some to be apostles, some to be prophets…" is found in Ephesians: **TRUE.** It is found in Ephesians 4.

5. The famous passage about the full armor (panoply) of God is found in Galatians: **FALSE.** It is found in Ephesians 6.

6. The passage, "I am astonished that you are so quickly abandoning the one who called you…" is found in Ephesians 1: **FALSE.** It is found in Galatians 1.

7. The yoke of slavery to the law is mentioned in Galatians 5: **TRUE**

8. "Awake, O sleeper! Rise from the dead, and Christ will shine on you" is thought by most scholars to be a baptismal hymn. It is found in Ephesians 5: **TRUE**

9. Which book follows Ephesians? **PHILIPPIANS**

10. The declaration, "From now on let no one cause me trouble, for I bear the marks [stigmata] of Jesus on my body," is found at the end of Galatians: **TRUE**

Bible Quiz 69: Philippians and Colossians

❶ These two letters each contain the same number of chapters. How many? ______________________________

❷ Who wrote them? ______________________________

❸ Both letters were directed to European churches: ❑ True or ❑ False?

❹ One theme of Philippians is:

❑ suffering ❑ joy ❑ prophecy ❑ the millennium

❺ A major theme of Colossians is ______________________________.

❑ the church ❑ the Holy Grail ❑ circumcision ❑ spiritual gifts

❻ Which book follows Colossians? ______________________________

❼ Where was the author when he penned these two letters?

❑ the Jerusalem Temple ❑ a Roman prison ❑ the Hierapolis Hilton ❑ Arabia

❽ "Let the word of Christ dwell in you richly" appears in Philippians 3:16: ❑ True or ❑ False?

❾ Philippians 1:21 reads, "For to me, to live is Christ, and to die is gain": ❑ True or ❑ False?

❿ The exhortation, "Be wise in the way you act towards outsiders," appears in Colossians 4: ❑ True or ❑ False?

Answers to Bible Quiz 69: Philippians and Colossians

1. These two letters each contain the same number of chapters. How many? **FOUR**

2. Who wrote them? **PAUL**

3. Both letters were directed to European churches: **FALSE.** Colosse is in Asia.

4. One theme of Philippians is: **JOY**

5. A major theme of Colossians is: **THE CHURCH**

6. Which book follows Colossians? **1 THESSALONIANS**

7. Where was the author when he penned these two letters? **A ROMAN PRISON**

8. "Let the word of Christ dwell in you richly" appears in Philippians 3:16: **FALSE.** It is Colossians 3:16.

9. Philippians 1:21 reads, "For to me, to live is Christ, and to die is gain": **TRUE**

10. The exhortation, "Be wise in the way you act towards outsiders," appears in Colossians 4: **TRUE**

Bible Quiz 70: 1 and 2 Thessalonians

❶ Who wrote these two letters?

❑ Paul ❑ Silas ❑ Timothy ❑ All the preceding

❷ How many chapters are in these two letters combined?

❑ 5 ❑ 8 ❑ 10 ❑ 15

❸ The "man of lawlessness" is mentioned in 1 Thessalonians:

❑ True or ❑ False?

❹ The idle (undisciplined) are to be warned, according to:

❑ 1 Thessalonians 5 ❑ 2 Thessalonians 3 ❑ both passages ❑ neither

❺ Thessalonica is in modern-day:

❑ Italy ❑ Greece ❑ Turkey ❑ none of the preceding

❻ No one can or should predict the end of the world, according to 1 Thessalonians 5: ❑ True or ❑ False?

❼ Which book follows 2 Thessalonians? ________________

❽ In which chapter of Acts is the Thessalonian church established?

❑ 15 ❑ 17 ❑ 19 ❑ 21

❾ Which chapter of 1 Thessalonians calls us to sexual purity?

❑ 3 ❑ 4 ❑ 5 ❑ 6

❿ "We were delighted to share with you not only the gospel of God, but our lives as well…":

❑ 1 Thessalonians 2:8 ❑ 2 Thessalonians 1:8 ❑ 1 Thessalonians 5:12

❑ 2 Thessalonians 5:12

Answers to Bible Quiz 70: 1 and 2 Thessalonians

1. Who wrote these two letters? **ALL THE PRECEDING**

2. How many chapters are in these two letters combined? **8**

3. The "man of lawlessness" is mentioned in 1 Thessalonians: **FALSE**

4. The idle (undisciplined) are to be warned, according to: **BOTH PASSAGES, 1 THESSALONIANS 5 AND 2 THESSALONIANS 3**

5. Thessalonica is in modern-day: **GREECE**

6. No one can or should predict the end of the word, according to 1 Thessalonians 5: **TRUE**

7. Which book follows 2 Thessalonians? **1 TIMOTHY**

8. In which chapter of Acts is the Thessalonian church established? **17**

9. Which chapter of 1 Thessalonians calls us to sexual purity? **4**

10. "We were delighted to share with you not only the gospel of God, but our lives as well...": **1 THESSALONIANS 2:8**

Bible Quiz 71: 1 and 2 Timothy

❶ Who wrote these two letters? ______________________________

❷ To whom were they written? ______________________________

❸ Which of the two letters is longer? _________________________

❹ To what city was 1 Timothy sent? __________________________

❺ What was Timothy's mother's name? ________________________

❻ In which chapter of Acts was Timothy recruited for the mission?

____

❼ "Watch your life and doctrine closely," appears in 1 Timothy chapter:

❑ 3 ❑ 4 ❑ 5 ❑ 6

❽ "Do your best to present yourself to God as one approved," appears in

2 Timothy chapter: ❑ 1 ❑ 2 ❑ 3 ❑ 4

❾ Which book follows 2 Timothy? _______________________________

❿ The statement, "Be strong in the grace," appears in:

❑ 1 Timothy 2 ❑ 2 Timothy 2

❑ 2 Timothy 5 ❑ None of the preceding

Answers to Bible Quiz 71: 1 and 2 Timothy

1. Who wrote these two letters? **PAUL**
2. To whom were they written? **TIMOTHY**
3. Which of the two letters is longer? **1 TIMOTHY**
4. To what city was 1 Timothy sent? **EPHESUS**
5. What was Timothy's mother's name? **EUNICE**
6. In which chapter of Acts was Timothy recruited for the mission? **16**
7. "Watch your life and doctrine closely" appears in 1 Timothy chapter: **4**
8. "Do your best to present yourself to God as one approved," appears in 2 Timothy chapter: **2**
9. Which book follows 2 Timothy? **TITUS**
10. The statement, "Be strong in the grace," appears in: **2 TIMOTHY 2**

Bible Quiz 72: Titus and Philemon

❶ Where was Titus ministering when Paul wrote him his letter?

____

❷ Titus was asked to appoint ________________ in every city.

❸ Philemon was a runaway slave: ❑ True or ❑ False?

❹ Philemon has only one chapter: ❑ True or ❑ False?

❺ Instructions for dealing with the divisive man are given in Titus chapter: ❑ 1 ❑ 2 ❑ 3 ❑ 4

❻ Instructions for silencing false teachers are given in Titus chapter: ❑ 1 ❑ 2 ❑ 3 ❑ 4

❼ Specific direction for older men, older women, younger men and younger women is given in Titus chapter: ❑ 1 ❑ 2 ❑ 3 ❑ 4

❽ Which book follows Philemon (in the standard order of most New Testaments)? ______________________________________

❾ Who was Onesimus? ________________________________

❿ Where was Paul when he wrote Philemon? ________________

Answers to Bible Quiz 72: Titus and Philemon

1. Where was Titus ministering when Paul wrote him his letter?

ON THE ISLAND OF CRETE

2. Titus was asked to appoint ____ in every city. **ELDERS**

3. Philemon was a runaway slave: **FALSE**

4. Philemon has only one chapter: **TRUE**

5. Instructions for dealing with the divisive man are given in Titus chapter: **3**

6. Instructions for silencing false teachers are given in Titus chapter: **1**

7. Specific direction for older men, older women, younger men and younger women is given in Titus chapter: **2**

8. Which book follows Philemon (in the standard order of most New Testaments)?

HEBREWS

9. Who was Onesimus? **THE RUNAWAY SLAVE**

10. Where was Paul when he wrote Philemon? **IN PRISON (IN ROME)**

Bible Quiz 73: Hebrews

❶ Who wrote Hebrews? ____________________________________

❷ This letter has 13 chapters: ❑ True or ❑ False?

❸ A major theme of the letter is the superiority of:

❑ the Hebrew language ❑ Christ ❑ the intellectual over the emotional

❑ Jews over Gentiles

❹ "The word of God is living and active…":

❑ 3:12 ❑ 4:12 ❑ 5:12 ❑ 6:12

❺ "Encourage one another…": ❑ 3:12 ❑ 4:12 ❑ 5:12 ❑ 6:12

❻ "We do not want you to become lazy…":

❑ 3:12 ❑ 4:12 ❑ 5:12 ❑ 6:12

❼ "By now you ought to be teachers…": ❑ 3:12 ❑ 4:12 ❑ 5:12 ❑ 6:12

❽ Jesus is a high priest, in the order of:

❑ Methuselah ❑ Mephibosheth ❑ Melchizedek ❑ Mephistopheles

❾ "And without faith it is impossible to please God…":

❑ 10:6 ❑ 11:6 ❑ 12:6 ❑ 13:6

❿ Which letter follows Hebrews? ______________________________

Answers to Bible Quiz 73: Hebrews

1. Who wrote Hebrews? **NO ONE KNOWS**

2. This letter has 13 chapters: **TRUE**

3. A major theme of the letter is the superiority of: **CHRIST**

4. "The word of God is living and active…" **4:12**

5. "Encourage one another..." **3:12**

6. "We do not want you to become lazy…" **6:12**

7. "By now you ought to be teachers…" **5:12**

8. Jesus is a high priest, in the order of: **MELCHIZEDEK**

9. "And without faith it is impossible to please God..." **11:6**

10. Which letter follows Hebrews? **JAMES** (in most Bibles)

Bible Quiz 74: James

❶ Who was James? ❑ The brother of John ❑ The brother of Jesus

❑ An apostle and one of the twelve ❑ All the preceding

❷ How many chapters are there in his letter? ❑ 3 ❑ 5 ❑ 7 ❑ 9

❸ Which book follows James? ______________________________

❹ How did James appear most prominently in the book of Acts?:

❑ He stood by while Stephen was martyred (Acts 8).

❑ He presided over the Jerusalem Council (Acts 15).

❑ He healed the lame man (Acts 3).

❑ He told Paul, "Your great learning is driving you insane" (Acts 26).

❺ Which chapter of James mentions orphans? ______________________

❻ Which chapter mentions confessing our sins to one another? ________

❼ James 3:6 warns, "The __________________ also is a fire, a world of evil among the parts of the body. It corrupts the whole person, sets the whole course of his life on fire, and is itself set on fire by hell."

❽ Which chapter warns businesspeople not to put their trust in business and business plans? ____

❾ James 2:26 reads, "As the body without the spirit is dead, so _______________________ without _____________________ is dead."

❿ James was executed in Jerusalem about 62 A.D.: ❑ True or ❑ False?

Answers to Bible Quiz 74: James

1. Who was James? **THE BROTHER OF JESUS**

2. How many chapters are there in his letter? **5**

3. Which book follows James? **1 PETER**

4. How did James appear most prominently in the book of Acts?

HE PRESIDED OVER THE JERUSALEM COUNCIL (Acts 15).

5. Which chapter of James mentions orphans? **ONE**

6. Which chapter mentions confessing our sins to one another? **FIVE**

7. James 3:6 warns, "The ________ also is a fire, a world of evil among the parts of the body. It corrupts the whole person, sets the whole course of his life on fire, and is itself set on fire by hell." **TONGUE**

8. Which chapter warns businesspeople not to put their trust in business and business plans? **FOUR**

9. James 2:26 reads, "As the body without the spirit is dead, so ________ without ________ is dead." **FAITH, DEEDS**

10. James was executed in Jerusalem about 62 A.D.: **TRUE**

Bible Quiz 75: 1 and 2 Peter

❶ Who wrote these two letters? ______________________________

❷ How many chapters do they contain in all? __________________

❸ Literary sensitivity question: Which of the two employs more colorful language? __________________

❹ Which set of three letters follows 1 and 2 Peter? __________________

❺ 2 Peter 2 warns of false prophets: ❑ True or ❑ False?

❻ 1 Peter 3 boldly states that baptism saves us: ❑ True or ❑ False?

❼ 2 Peter 1 warns of the need to repent before the coming of the Lord: ❑ True or ❑ False?

❽ 1 Peter 2 calls us to walk in Christ's footsteps and be willing to suffer: ❑ True or ❑ False?

❾ In 2 Peter 1, the apostle speaks of his imminent death: ❑ True or ❑ False?

❿ Two-part question: Since Peter was executed in 64 A.D., what is the latest year these letters can have been written? Who was the emperor that year? ____

Answers to Bible Quiz 75: 1 and 2 Peter

1. Who wrote these two letters? **PETER**

2. How many chapters do they contain in all? **EIGHT**

3. Literary sensitivity question: Which of the two employs more colorful language? **2 PETER, BY FAR** (in the original Greek as well as in translation)

4. Which set of three letters follows 1-2 Peter? **1-3 JOHN**

5. 2 Peter 2 warns of false prophets: **TRUE**

6. 1 Peter 3 boldly states that baptism saves us: **TRUE**

7. 2 Peter 1 warns of the need to repent before the coming of the Lord: **FALSE.** (That warning is in 2 Peter 3.)

8. 1 Peter 2 calls us to walk in Christ's footsteps and be willing to suffer: **TRUE**

9. In 2 Peter 1, the apostle speaks of his imminent death: **TRUE**

10. Two-part question: Since Peter was executed in 64 A.D., what is the latest year these letters can have been written? Who was the emperor that year?
64 A.D., OF COURSE. NERO WAS ON THE THRONE (UNTIL HIS SUICIDE IN 68)

Bible Quiz 76: 1, 2 and 3 John

❶ The apostle John is traditionally thought to have been the author of these three letters: ❑ True or ❑ False?

❷ Which of these three letters have only one chapter? ________________

For questions 3—8, identify the letter in which each quotation or name appears.

❸ "The deceiver and the antichrist": 1 John, 2 John or 3 John?

____

❹ Diotrephes and Demetrius: 1 John, 2 John or 3 John? ______________

❺ "The elect lady" / "your chosen sister": 1 John, 2 John or 3 John?

____

❻ "Do not love the world…": 1 John, 2 John or 3 John? ______________

❼ Gaius: 1 John, 2 John or 3 John? ______________________________

❽ "Test the spirits": 1 John, 2 John or 3 John? ____________________

❾ Which book follows 3 John? ___________________________________

❿ Which other two New Testament documents have the same general style and themes as 1-3 John? ______________________________

Answers to Bible Quiz 76: 1, 2 and 3 John

1. The apostle John is traditionally thought to have been the author of these three letters: **TRUE**

2. Which of these three letters have only one chapter? **2 AND 3 JOHN**

For questions 3 through 8, identify the letter in which each statement or name appears.

3. The deceiver and the antichrist: **2 JOHN**

4. Diotrephes and Demetrius: **3 JOHN**

5. "The elect lady" / "your chosen sister": **2 JOHN**

6. "Do not love the world...": **1 JOHN**

7. Gaius: **3 JOHN**

8. "Test the spirits": **1 JOHN**

9. Which book follows 3 John? **JUDE**

10. Which other two New Testament documents have the same general style and themes as 1-3 John? **JOHN (THE GOSPEL) AND REVELATION**

Bible Quiz 77: Jude and Revelation

❶ Who was Jude? ❑ The brother of Jesus ❑ An apostle ❑ A Beatle

❑ All the preceding

❷ How many chapters are there in Revelation? ❑ 16 ❑ 22 ❑ 31 ❑ 44

❸ What is the other name for the book of Revelation?

❑ The Apocrypha ❑ The Scary Bible Book ❑ The Apostrophe

❑ The Apocalypse

❹ Which books of the Bible are Jude and Revelation?

❑ 63rd and 64th ❑ 65th and 66th ❑ 67th and 68th ❑ 69th and 70th

❺ "Wild waves of the sea": Jude or Revelation? ________________

❻ "The great white throne": Jude or Revelation? ________________

❼ "The faith once for all delivered to the saints": Jude or Revelation?

____

❽ "Neither hot nor cold": Jude or Revelation? ________________

❾ How many churches does Jesus address in Revelation 2-3?

____

❿ Revelation alludes or quotes ________________ hundreds of times.

❑ Greco-Roman writers ❑ The Old Testament

❑ The four gospels ❑ Plato and Aristotle

Answers to Bible Quiz 77: Jude and Revelation

1. Who was Jude? **THE BROTHER OF JESUS**
2. How many chapters are there in Revelation? **22**
3. What is the other name for the book of Revelation? **THE APOCALYPSE**
4. Which books of the Bible are Jude and Revelation? **65TH AND 66TH**
5. "Wild waves of the sea": **JUDE**
6. "The great white throne": **REVELATION**
7. "The faith once for all delivered to the saints": **JUDE**
8. "Neither hot nor cold": **REVELATION**
9. How many churches does Jesus address in Revelation 2-3? **SEVEN**
10. Revelation alludes or quotes hundreds of times. **THE OLD TESTAMENT**

ANSWERS

Bible Quiz 78: Old Testament Chronology

Place the following biblical events in chronological order:

A. King David rules Israel

B. Esther speaks up and saves her people

C. Solomon answers the questions of the Queen of Sheba

D. Moses receives the Law at Sinai

E. Joseph is sold into slavery

F. Joshua fights the battle of Jericho

____

____

____

____

____

____

Answers to Bible Quiz 78: Old Testament Chronology

Here are the biblical events in chronological order:

E. Joseph is sold into slavery (around 1900 B.C.)

D. Moses receives the Law at Sinai (around 1450 B.C.)

F. Joshua fights the battle of Jericho (around 1400 B.C.)

A. King David rules Israel (around 1000 B.C.)

C. Solomon answers the questions of the Queen of Sheba (around 950 B.C.)

B. Esther speaks up and saves her people (around 450 B.C.)

Bible Quiz 79: New Testament Chronology

Place the following biblical events in chronological order:

A. Jesus rises from the dead

B. Paul is executed

C. 1 Thessalonians is written

D. John the Baptist challenges Herod on his sexual immorality

E. Elizabeth becomes pregnant

F. Paul is shipwrecked on Malta

G. Cornelius is baptized

Answers to Bible Quiz 79: New Testament Chronology

The following biblical events in chronological order:

E. Elizabeth becomes pregnant (6 B.C.)

D. John the Baptist challenges Herod on his sexual immorality (27 A.D.)

A. Jesus rises from the dead (30 A.D.)

G. Cornelius is baptized (40A.D.?)

C. 1 Thessalonians is written (50 A.D.)

F. Paul is shipwrecked on Malta (58 A.D.)

B. Paul is executed (65-68 A.D.)

Bible Quiz 80: Chronology of Jesus' Life, Part 1

Place the following biblical events in chronological order:

A. Great Commission

B. Walking on water

C. Ascension at Bethany

D. Circumcision

E. Peter's confession at Caesarea Philippi

F. Appearance to Thomas

G. Refuses to answer Herod

Answers to Bible Quiz 80: Chronology of Jesus' Life, Pt 1

The following biblical events in chronological order:

D. Circumcision

B. Walking on water

E. Peter's confession at Caesarea Philippi

G. Refuses to answer Herod

F. Appearance to Thomas

A. Great Commission

C. Ascension at Bethany

Bible Quiz 81: Chronology of Jesus' Life, Part 2

Place the following biblical events in chronological order:

A. Ascension

B. Incarnation

C. Resurrection

D. Parousia (Return)

E. Baptism

F. Transfiguration

G. Crucifixion

____

____

____

____

____

____

____

Answers to Bible Quiz 81: Chronology of Jesus' Life, Pt 2

The following biblical events in chronological order:

B. Incarnation

E. Baptism

F. Transfiguration

G. Crucifixion

C. Resurrection

A. Ascension

D. Parousia (Return)

Bible Quiz 82: Chronology of the Kings of Israel

Place the following kings in chronological order:

A. Manasseh

B. Solomon

C. Josiah

D. David

E. Saul

F. Rehoboam

G. Zedekiah

Answers to Bible Quiz 82: Chronology of the Kings of Israel

The following kings in chronological order:

E. SAUL

D. DAVID

B. SOLOMON

F. REHOBOAM

A. MANASSEH

C. JOSIAH

G. ZEDEKIAH

Bible Quiz 83: Translation of the Bible

1. What is a translation? ______________________________

____

2. What is a transliteration? ______________________________

3. Which world language has the greatest number of Bible versions? ___

____

4. What is a paraphrase? ______________________________

____

5. Arrange the following in order of date of translation:

A. Revised Standard Version

B. Tyndale

C. Holman Christian Standard Bible

D. New International Version

E. King James Version

____

____

____

____

____

____

Answers to Bible Quiz 83: Translation of the Bible

1. What is a translation? **A BIBLE VERSION RENDERED WORD BY WORD OR THOUGHT BY THOUGHT FROM THE ORIGINAL HEBREW/ ARAMAIC (OLD TESTAMENT) OR GREEK (NEW TESTAMENT) INTO ANOTHER LANGUAGE**

2. What is a transliteration? **THE TRANSCRIPTION OF A WORD FROM ITS ORIGINAL LANGUAGE INTO THE LETTERS OF ANOTHER LANGUAGE.** For example, "diakonos" (servant) became deacon; "baptisma" (immersion) became baptism.

3. Which world language has the greatest number of Bible versions? **ENGLISH, BY FAR (MORE THAN 100 VERSIONS)**

4. What is a paraphrase? **A FREE RENDERING OF THE THOUGHT OF A BIBLICAL BOOK ACCORDING TO THE UNDERSTANDING OF THE PARAPHRASER. THIS IS NOT A TRANSLATION.** (For example, *The Message*)

5. Arrange the following in order of date of translation:

TYNDALE—1500s

KING JAMES VERSION—1600s

REVISED STANDARD Version—COMPLETED 1952

NEW INTERNATIONAL VERSION—COMPLETED 1978

HOLMAN CHRISTIAN STANDARD BIBLE—COMPLETED 1999

Bible Quiz 84: Literary Genres of the Bible

Match the biblical book with its literary genre:

Leviticus _______________	A. EPISTLE
1 Samuel _______________	B. NARRATIVE
Proverbs _______________	C. PROPHECY
Amos _______________	D. APOCALYPSE
Mark _______________	E. LAW
Jude _______________	F. WISDOM LITERATURE
Revelation _______________	G. GOSPEL

Answers to Bible Quiz 84: Literary Genres of the Bible

Match the biblical book with its literary genre:

Leviticus—	E. LAW
1 Samuel—	B. NARRATIVE
Proverbs—	F. WISDOM LITERATURE
Amos—	C. PROPHECY
Mark—	G. GOSPEL
Jude—	A. EPISTLE
Revelation—	D. APOCALYPSE

Bible Quiz 85: Authors of the Bible

Match the biblical book with its author. Since some books were written by more than one person, in some cases the correct answer will be the dominant or most eminent writer.

Ecclesiastes ________________	A. DAVID
Numbers ________________	B. PAUL
Acts ___________________	C. MICAH
Titus ___________________	D. JOHN
Psalms __________________	E. MOSES
Micah __________________	F. SOLOMON
Revelation ________________	G. LUKE

Answers to Bible Quiz 85: Authors of the Bible

Match the biblical book with its author. Since some books were written by more than one person, in some cases the correct answer will be the dominant or most eminent writer.

Ecclesiastes—	F. SOLOMON
Numbers—	E. MOSES
Acts—	G. LUKE
Titus —	B. PAUL
Psalms—	A. DAVID
Micah—	C. MICAH
Revelation—	D. JOHN

Bible Quiz 86: Numbers of the Bible

Match the following numbers with the biblical books to which they relate.

144,000 ____________	A. Exodus
153 ________________	B. Matthew—Revelation
603,550 ____________	C. John
666 ________________	D. A man's number, the number of the beast (Revelation 13)
1 __________________	E. Revelation
260 ________________	F. Judges
1,100 ______________	G. Throughout the Bible

Answers to Bible Quiz 86: Numbers of the Bible

Match the following numbers with the biblical books to which they relate.

144,000—E. REVELATION: Symbolic number of the redeemed in heaven (Revelation 7, 14)

153—C. JOHN: The number of fish hauled ashore (John 21)

603,550—A. EXODUS: The number of Israelite soldiers (Exodus 38, Numbers 1)

666—D. A MAN'S NUMBER, THE NUMBER OF THE BEAST (REVELATION 13)

1–G. THROUGHOUT THE BIBLE: That's right, it's everywhere, appearing more than 2,700 times!

260—B. MATTHEW-REVELATION: The number of chapters in the New Testament

1,100—F. JUDGES: The number of pieces of silver (Judges 16, 17)

Bible Quiz 87: Cities of the Bible

❶ Which famous city was controlled by the Jebusites before David's army took possession of it? ______________________

❷ How many Antiochs are there in the New Testament? ____________

❸ How many Caesareas are there in the New Testament? ____________

❹ What was the population of Ai, the second largest city in Canaan (before the Israelites took the Promised Land)?

❑ 2000 ❑ 12,000 ❑ 120,000 ❑ 1,200,000

❺ Which OT city had a population of 120,000?

❑ Nineveh ❑ Jerusalem ❑ Jericho ❑ Babylon

❻ What was the largest city of the Roman Empire (population 1 million)?

❑ Jerusalem ❑ Athens ❑ Rome ❑ Alexandria

❼ King Jeroboam of Israel (who lived in the 10th century B.C.) established centers for false worship in the cities of Dan and:

❑ Bethel ❑ Bethlehem ❑ Beth Shemesh ❑ Bethuel

❽ Approximately how many times does the word "city" appear in the Bible? ❑ 8 ❑ 80 ❑ 800 ❑ 8000

❾ How many Cities of Refuge were allocated for protection from avengers of blood in ancient Israelite times? ❑ 2 ❑ 6 ❑ 66 ❑ 144

❿ Jerusalem was (and is) in the north of Israel: ❑ True or ❑ False?

Answers to Bible Quiz 87: Cities of the Bible

1. Which famous city was controlled by the Jebusites before David's army took possession of it? **JERUSALEM**

2. How many Antiochs are there in the New Testament? **TWO** (Syrian Antioch, the larger of the two, and Pisidian Antioch. See the book of Acts.)

3. How many Caesareas are there in the New Testament? **TWO** (Caesarea Maritima, headquarters of Pontius Pilate, and Caesarea Philippi, where Jesus asked, "Who do people say I am?")

4. What was the population of Ai, the second largest city in Canaan (before the Israelites took the Promised Land)? **12,000** (Joshua 8:25)

5. Which OT city had a population of 120,000? **NINEVEH** (Jonah 4:11)

6. What was the largest city of the Roman Empire (population 1 million)? **ROME**

7. King Jeroboam of Israel (who lived in the 10th century B.C.) established centers for false worship in the cities of Dan and: **BETHEL**

8. Approximately how many times does the word "city" appear in the Bible? **800 TIMES**

9. How many Cities of Refuge were allocated for protection from avengers of blood in ancient Israelite times? **6**

10. Jerusalem was (and is) in the north of Israel. **FALSE**

Bible Quiz 88: The Land of the Bible, Part 1

❶ Which country is NOT mentioned in the Bible?

❑ Edom ❑ India ❑ China ❑ Libya

❷ In which country did Jesus, Joseph, Moses and Jeroboam all reside, at one time or another? ______________________________

❸ The Dead Sea is larger than the Sea of Galilee: ❑ True or ❑ False?

❹ The Dead Sea and the Sea of Galilee are both fresh water bodies:

❑ True or ❑ False?

❺ What is the name for the southern desert of Israel? ____________

❻ Place the following cities in order, from north to south: Jerusalem, Dan Shechem: ______________________________

❼ It never snows in Israel: ❑ True or ❑ False?

❽ What was the western boundary of the Promised Land? __________

❾ Place the following cities in order from east to west: Jericho, Jerusalem, Gaza ______________________________

❿ Figs, olives and grapes all grow in Israel. ❑ True or ❑ False?

Answers to Bible Quiz 88: The Land of the Bible, Pt 1

1. Which country is NOT mentioned in the Bible? **CHINA**

2. In which country did Jesus, Joseph, Moses and Jeroboam all reside, at one time or another? **EGYPT**

3. The Dead Sea is larger than the Sea of Galilee: **TRUE**

4. The Dead Sea and the Sea of Galilee are both fresh water bodies: **FALSE.** The Dead Sea is salt water, the Sea of Galilee fresh water.

5. What is the name for the southern desert of Israel? **THE NEGEV**

6. Place the following cities in order, from north to south: Jerusalem, Dan, Shechem: **DAN—SHECHEM—JERUSALEM**

7. It never snows in Israel: **FALSE**

8. What was the western boundary of the Promised Land?
THE MEDITERRANEAN SEA

9. Place the following cities in order from east to west: Jericho, Jerusalem, Gaza
JERICHO-JERUSALEM-GAZA

10. Figs, olives, pomegranates and grapes all grow in Israel. **TRUE**

ANSWERS

Bible Quiz 89: The Land of the Bible, Part 2

❶ "Israel" was the covenant name of which of the patriarchs of Genesis?

____

❷ The word "Palestine" comes from the word for Philistine:

❑ True or ❑ False?

❸ Today, the Jordan River forms part of the border between Israel and Jordan: ❑ True or ❑ False?

❹ The cities of Canaan that the book of Joshua says were burned to the ground were Ai and ______________________ (in the south) and Hazor (in the north).

❺ The book of Joshua states that the population of Ai, at the time of its destruction (around 1400 B.C.) was:

❑ 12,000 ❑ 120,000 ❑ 1,200,000 ❑ 12,000,000

❻ The Tabernacle of the Lord was at Shiloh before it was in Jerusalem:

❑ True or ❑ False?

❼ David reigned 33 years in Jerusalem after reigning approximately 7.5 years in ____

❽ Where did most of the Philistines settle?

❑ The Coastal Plain ❑ The Hill Country

❑ The Jordan Valley ❑ Transjordan

❾ Place the following three kingdoms in order, from east to west: Egypt, Babylonia, Israel

____

❿ Technically speaking, the Canaanites lived in Canaan:

❑ True or ❑ False?

Answers to Bible Quiz 89: The Land of the Bible, Pt 2

1. "Israel" was the covenant name of which of the patriarchs of Genesis? **JACOB**

2. The word "Palestine" comes from the word for Philistine: **TRUE**

3. Today, the Jordan River forms part of the border between Israel and Jordan: **TRUE**

4. The cities of Canaan that the book of Joshua says were burned to the ground were Ai and ___ (in the south) and Hazor (in the north). **JERICHO**

5. The book of Joshua states that the population of Ai, at the time of its destruction (around 1400 B.C.) was: **12,000** (see Joshua 8:25)

6. The Tabernacle of the Lord was at Shiloh before it was in Jerusalem: **TRUE**

7. David reigned 33 years in Jerusalem after reigning 7.5 years in: **HEBRON**

8. Where did most of the Philistines settle? **THE COASTAL PLAIN**

9. Place the following three kingdoms in order, from east to west: Egypt, Babylonia, Israel: **BABYLONIA—ISRAEL—EGYPT**

10. Technically speaking, the Canaanites lived in Canaan: **TRUE** (of course!)

ANSWERS

Bible Quiz 90: Brothers of the Bible

❶ Who was Simon Peter's brother? ______________________

❷ Who was Abel's unloving brother? ______________________

❸ ❹ Name the brothers (apostles) dubbed "Sons of Thunder" by Jesus.

____

____

❺ ❻ ❼ ❽ Jesus had four brothers (Matthew 13). Name them!

____

____

____

____

❾ Who was the father of the brothers Joseph, Benjamin and Gad?

____

❿ Jesus is called our "brother" in the New Testament: ❑ True or ❑ False?

Answers to Bible Quiz 90: Brothers of the Bible

1. Who was Simon Peter's brother? **ANDREW**

2. Who was Abel's unloving brother? **CAIN**

3-4. Name the brothers (apostles) dubbed "Sons of Thunder" by Jesus.

JAMES AND JOHN

5-9. Jesus had four brothers, according to Matthew 13. Name them!

JAMES, JOSEPH, SIMON AND JUDAS

9. Who was the father of the brothers Joseph, Benjamin and Gad?

JACOB (ISRAEL)

10. Jesus is called our "brother" in the New Testament: **TRUE** (Hebrews 2:11)

Bible Quiz 91: Land Animals of the Bible

1 To which two animals does Jesus refer in Matthew 7:6?

____

2 In Old Testament law, what animal was allowed as an alternative to lamb for the Passover meal? ______________________________

3 Which kind of animal did Jesus ride on in the "Triumphal Entry," in which he fulfilled the prophecy of Zechariah 9:9? ______________

4 What do the camel and the pig have in common, in light of the Torah?

____

5 "Don't muzzle the ____________ while it is treading out the grain."

6 Are tigers found anywhere in the Bible? How about unicorns?

____

7 Which animal is mentioned in Song of Songs 2, and again (in reference to Herod) in Luke 13? ______________________________

8 In Numbers, we find a talking donkey. Whom was she addressing?

____

9 2 Peter 2 warns of the perils of being drawn back into the world. Which animals are used as illustrations? ______________________

10 A small, shy, furry mammal is mentioned a number of times in the Old Testament. It is called a coney. What are its other names? __________

____

Answers to Bible Quiz 91: Land Animals of the Bible

1. To which two animals does Jesus refer in Matthew 7:6? **DOGS AND PIGS**
2. In Old Testament law, what animal was allowed as an alternative to lamb for the Passover meal? **GOAT**
3. Which kind of animal did Jesus ride on in the "Triumphal Entry," in which he fulfilled the prophecy of Zechariah 9:9? **DONKEY**
4. What do the camel and the pig have in common, in light of the Torah? **BOTH ARE UNCLEAN**
5. "Don't muzzle the ____ while it is treading out the grain." **OX**
6. Are tigers found anywhere in the Bible? How about unicorns? **TIGERS: NO. UNICORNS: NO, ALTHOUGH THEY DO APPEAR IN THE KJV VERSION OF 1611.**
7. Which animal is mentioned in Song of Songs 2, and again (in reference to Herod) in Luke 13? **FOX**
8. In Numbers, we find a talking donkey. Whom was she addressing? **BALAAM**
9. 2 Peter 2 warns of the perils of being drawn back into the world. Which animals are used as illustrations? **DOGS AND PIGS** (Again!)
10. A small, shy, furry mammal is mentioned a number of times in the Old Testament. It is called a coney. What are its other names? **HYRAX AND ROCK BADGER**

Bible Quiz 92: Sea Animals of the Bible

❶ What do the eel and the lobster have in common?

____

❷ The end of the book of Job poetically depicts which animal?

____

❸ How many species of saltwater fish inhabit the Sea of Galilee?

____

❹ Who is found cooking fish for his followers in John 21?

____

❺ How large was the catch in John 21 once Peter and crew followed the Master's advice?

____

❻ The Bible says explicitly that Jonah was swallowed by a whale:

❑ True or ❑ False?

❼ Which aquatic mammal gave its skin for the furnishings of the Tabernacle? ______________________________

❽ What unusual item was once found in a fish's mouth in Matthew 17?

____

❾ What is the biblical name for various (larger) sea creatures?

____

❿ The Flood wiped out all fish: ❑ True or ❑ False?

Answers to Bible Quiz 92: Sea Animals of the Bible

1. What do the eel and the lobster have in common? **THEY ARE UNCLEAN FOODS**

2. The end of the book of Job poetically depicts which animal? **THE CROCODILE**

3. How many species of saltwater fish inhabit the Sea of Galilee? **NONE—THIS BODY OF WATER IS FRESH**

4. Who is found cooking fish for his followers in John 21? **JESUS**

5. How large was the catch in John 21 once Peter and crew followed the Master's advice? **153 FISH**

6. The Bible explicitly says Jonah was swallowed by a whale: **FALSE. HE BIBLE ONLY SAYS "DAG GADOL, OR BIG FISH." THIS COULD BE A WHALE, GROUPER, OR A NUMBER OF OTHER AQUATIC CREATURES**

7. Which aquatic mammal gave its skin for the furnishings of the Tabernacle? **A SEA COW OR MANATEE**

8. What unusual item was once found in a fish's mouth in Matthew 17? **A COIN (A STATER, OR FOUR-DRACHMA PIECE, TO MAKE JESUS' AND PETER'S TEMPLE TAX PAYMENT).**

9. What is the biblical name for various (larger) sea creatures? **LEVIATHAN**

10. The Flood wiped out all fish: **FALSE**

ANSWERS

Bible Quiz 93: Air Animals of the Bible

❶ What sort of bird fed the prophet Elijah in the book of 1 Kings?

____

❷ What do the following have in common: seagull, owl, bat?

____

❸ Which bird, according to Jesus, does not fall to the ground apart from our Father's knowledge? _______________________________

❹ "Where the dead body is found, there the _______________ will gather."

❺ Jesus compares himself to a mother hen: ❑ True or ❑ False?

❻ Who released a dove and a raven?

____

❼ On which "creation day" were the birds made in Genesis 1?

____

❽ Approximately how many times does the word "bird(s)" appear in the Bible? ____

❾ The phoenix is found in the Bible: ❑ True or ❑ False?

❿ The peacock is found in the Bible: ❑ True or ❑ False?

Answers to Bible Quiz 93: Air Animals of the Bible

1. What sort of bird fed the prophet Elijah in the book of 1 Kings? **RAVENS**

2. What do the following have in common: seagull, owl, bat? **THEY ARE UNCLEAN**

3. Which bird, according to Jesus, does not fall to the ground apart from our Father's knowledge? **SPARROW**

4. "Where the dead body is found, there the ____ will gather." **VULTURES**

5. Jesus compares himself to a mother hen: **TRUE (MATTHEW 23:37, LUKE 13:34)**

6. Who released a dove and a raven? **NOAH**

7. On which "creation day" were the birds made in Genesis 1? **DAY 5**

8. Approximately how many times does the word "bird(s)" appear in the Bible? **140 TIMES (NAS)**

9. The phoenix is found in the Bible: **FALSE.** Although "PHOINIX" does appear a couple of times. This word means not only the mythological creature (of interest these days to all the Harry Potter fans) but also to the Palm tree. (See Psalm 91:13 and Joel 1:12.)

10. The peacock is found in the Bible: **TRUE** (1 Kings 10:22 and 2 Chronicles 9:21)

Bible Quiz 94: The Kings of Israel

❶ Who was the first king of Israel? ______________________

❷ Who was his successor? ______________________

❸ Under whose kingship was Israel formally split into two kingdoms, North and South? Hint: His name begins with an "'R".

____

❹ The Northern Kingdom of Israel was taken into captivity in the 8th century B.C. Which foreign power did this?

❑ Egypt ❑ Assyria ❑ Babylon ❑ Persia

❺ Which king was married to Jezebel? ______________________

❻ Which king of Israel fired only three "arrows of victory" out of a window in the presence of Elisha?______________________

❼ Who was the first king to preside over the Northern Kingdom of Israel (after the split)?

____

❽ Who was the third king of Israel?______________________

❾ Approximately how many primary and secondary wives (concubines) did this man have?______________________

❿ Which Israelite king reigned only seven days?

____

Answers to Bible Quiz 94: The Kings of Israel

1. Who was the first king of Israel? **SAUL**

2. Who was his successor? **DAVID**

3. Under whose kingship was Israel formally split into two kingdoms, North and South? Hint: His name begins with an "R.". **REHOBOAM**

4. The Northern Kingdom of Israel was taken into captivity in the 8th century B.C. Which foreign power did this? **ASSYRIA**

5. Which king was married to Jezebel? **AHAB**

6. Which king of Israel fired only three "arrows of victory" out of a window in the presence of Elisha? **JOASH**

7. Who was the first king to preside over the Northern Kingdom of Israel (after the split)? **JEROBOAM (JEROBOAM I)**

8. Who was the third king of Israel? **SOLOMON**

9. Approximately how many primary and secondary wives (concubines) did this man have? **1,000**

10. Which Israelite king reigned only seven days? **ZIMRI**

ANSWERS

Bible Quiz 95: The Kings of Judah

❶ Which was the southern kingdom, Israel or Judah? ______________

❷ Who was the first Judean king of the divided kingdom?

____

❸ Under whose reign was the long-lost Book of the Law discovered?

____

❹ Whose prayer and faith repulsed the armies of Assyria in 701 B.C.?

____

❺ What is the significance of the year 587 B.C.?

____

❻ Which foreign power had been asserting itself in the ancient near east since the 600s B.C.? ______________

❼ And who had been sitting as king (the final monarch) in that year?

____

❽ How many kings in all reigned in Jerusalem, starting with Saul?

❑ 12 ❑ 22 ❑ 32

❾ Which Judean king burned the scroll of Jeremiah in the fire, as recorded in Jeremiah 36? ______________

❿ Who reigned for 55 years, committed horrendous atrocities and acts of spiritual infidelity—yet genuinely turned to God at the very end of his life? ______________

Answers to Bible Quiz 95: The Kings of Judah

1. Which was the southern kingdom, Israel or Judah? **JUDAH**

2. Who was the first Judean king of the divided kingdom? **REHOBOAM**

3. Under whose reign was the long-lost Book of the Law discovered? **JOSIAH**

4. Whose prayer and faith repulsed the armies of Assyria in 701 B.C.? **HEZEKIAH**

5. What is the significance of the year 587 B.C.? **THIS WAS THE YEAR THE SOUTHERN KINGDOM OF JUDAH FELL.**

6. Which foreign power had been asserting itself in the ancient near east since the 600s B.C.? **BABYLON**

7. And who had been sitting as king (the final monarch) in that year? **ZEDEKIAH**

8. How many kings in all reigned in Jerusalem, starting with Saul? **22**

9. Which Judean king burned the scroll of Jeremiah in the fire, as recorded in Jeremiah 36? **JEHOIAKIM**

10. Who reigned for 55 years, committed horrendous atrocities and acts of spiritual infidelity—yet genuinely turned to God at the very end of his life? **MANASSEH**

Bible Quiz 96: Kings of the Nations

❶ In biblical times, what were the kings of Egypt called?

____

❷ Properly spell this word—if you haven't already done so in question 1!

____

❸ Which Persian king was husband to Esther? ______________

❹ On which continent does one find Egypt? ______________

❺ On which continent would one have found Assyria, Babylon and Persia? ______________

❻ Which Babylonian king seems to have suffered from lycanthropy or some other rare disorder? (He ate grass!)

____

❼ Which nation did the following kings rule: Shalaneser, Tiglath-Pileser, and Sargon? ______________

❽ Which nation did Belshazzar rule (apparently as second-in-command to Nabonidus, in the 6th century B.C.)? ______________

____

❾ What is the modern name of the nation whose ancient borders (more or less) were those of Persia?______________

❿ Nahum and Jonah are two books of the Bible demonstrating God's love for the nations—in this case, the nation of ______________

______________________________.

Answers to Bible Quiz 96: Kings of the Nations

1. In biblical times, what were the kings of Egypt called? **PHAROAHS**

2. Properly spell this word—if you haven't already done so in question 1! **P-H-A-R-A-O-H**

3. Which Persian king was husband to Esther? **XERXES (AHASUERUS)**

4. On which continent does one find Egypt? **AFRICA**

5. On which continent would one have found Assyria, Babylon and Persia? **ASIA**

6. Which Babylonian king seems to have suffered from lycanthropy or some other rare disorder? (He ate grass!) **NEBUCHADNEZZAR**

7. Which nation did the following kings rule: Shalaneser, Tiglath-Pileser, and Sargon? **ASSYRIA**

8. Which nation did Belshazzar rule (apparently as second-in-command to Nabonidus, in the 6th century B.C.)? **BABYLON**

9. What is the modern name of the nation whose ancient borders (more or less) were those of Persia? **IRAN**

10. Nahum and Jonah are two books of the Bible demonstrating God's love for the nations—in this case, the nation of____. **ASSYRIA**

Bible Quiz 97: Roman Leaders

❶ Who was emperor when Jesus Christ was born, according to Luke?

____

❷ Who was governor of Judea when Jesus was crucified?

____

❸ What was the name of the half-Jewish, half-Idumean (Edomite) Roman puppet ruling in Galilee?

____

❹ When did the armies of General Pompey take over in the Middle East?

❑ 363 B.C. ❑ 63 B.C. ❑ 23 A.D.

❺ In the Roman army, what was the title of the officer in charge of 100 men? ____________________________________

❻ Can you name one such officer? Hint: Acts 10.

____

❼ What is the word used to describe all emperors of Rome after Julius?

____

❽ Can you think of any modern words or terms deriving from this word?

____

❾ Who was the Roman emperor who presided over the Council of Nicaea in 325 A.D.? Hint: He delayed his baptism until he was on his deathbed, in case he might sin. __________________________

❿ Who was the nastiest and most infamous of the Roman emperors? Hint: He fiddled while Rome burned. ____________________

Answers to Bible Quiz 97: Roman Leaders

1. Who was emperor when Jesus Christ was born, according to Luke? **TIBERIUS**

2. Who was governor of Judea when Jesus was crucified? **PILATE**

3. What was the name of the half-Jewish, half-Idumean (Edomite) Roman puppet ruling in Galilee? **HEROD**

4. When did the armies of General Pompey take over in the Middle East? **63 B.C.**

5. In the Roman army, what was the name of the officer in charge of 100 men? **CENTURION**

6. Can you name one such officer? Hint: Acts 10. **CORNELIUS**

7. What is the word used to describe all emperors of Rome after Julius? **CAESAR**

8. Can you think of any modern words or terms deriving from this word? **CAESAR SALAD, CZAR** (also spelled Csar, Tzar and Tsar), **KAISER** (as in Kaiser Wilhelm II)

9. Who was the Roman emperor who presided over the Council of Nicaea in 325 A.D.? Hint: He delayed his baptism until he was on his deathbed, in case he might sin. **CONSTANTINE**

10. Who was the nastiest and most infamous of the Roman emperors? Hint: He fiddled while Rome burned. **NERO**

Bible Quiz 98: King David

❶ David, son of ________, son of ________, son of ________ wife of ________

❷ How many brothers did David have? ____________ Name two (more for extra credit). ____________________________________

❸ Name David's wives. ____

❹ Name three of David's sons. ____

❺ Jonathan's lame son's was______________ Hint: 2 Samuel 4:4. (Extra point if you spell it correctly!)

❻ Before David fought Goliath, he was Saul's armor bearer: ❑ True or ❑ False?

❼. ________________ the Edomite told Saul that ________________ the priest had helped David, so Saul had the priest's family murdered.

❽ Nabal means: ____

❾ When David was afraid of _______, King of Gath, he escaped by __________.

❿ What was Adullam? ____

⓫ Match the commander to the king:

David	Abner
Saul	Joab

⓬ The Amalekites raided the city of ___________and carried off David's family.

⓭ The King of Israel after Saul was _______________ (not David!)

⓮ Who was Uriah? ____

⓯ Who said, "You are the man"? ______________________________________

⓰ Who was David's daughter who was raped? ____________________________

⓱ Who was Ahithophel? Hint: 2 Samuel 16:23. _________________________

⓲ Who cursed David and threw rocks at him? ___________________________

⓳ Which son of David tried to steal the throne from him? __________________

⓴ Which books of the Bible describe the life of David? ____________________

Answers to Bible Quiz 98: King David

1. David, son of **JESSE,** son of **OBED**, son of **RUTH**, wife of **BOAZ.**
2. How many brothers did David have? **SEVEN**
Name two (more for extra credit, one point apiece). **ELIAB, SHAMMAH, ABINADAB**.
3. Name David's wives: **MICHAL, ABIGAIL, AHINOAM, BATHSHEBA**
4. Name three of David's sons. **ABSALOM, AMNON, SOLOMON**
5. Jonathan's lame son's was: **MEPHIBOSHETH** (2 Samuel 4:4)
6. Before David fought Goliath, he was Saul's armor bearer: **TRUE**
7. _____ the Edomite told Saul that _____ the priest had helped David, so Saul had the priest's family murdered. **DOEG, AHIMELECH**
8. Nabal means: **FOOL**
9. When David was afraid of _____, King of Gath, he escaped by _____.
ACHISH, FEIGNING INSANITY.
10. What was Adullam? **THE CAVE WHERE DAVID MET WITH THOSE WHO WERE IN DEBT, DISTRESSED AND DISCONTENT, AND HE BECAME THEIR LEADER** (1 Samuel 22).
11. Match the commander to the king: **DAVID AND JOAB**
SAUL AND ABNER
12. The Amalekites raided the city of _____ and carried off David's family.
ZIKLAG
13. The King of Israel after Saul was _____. **ISH-BOSHETH** (2 Samuel 2:8)
14. Who was Uriah? **URIAH THE HITTITE, A MIGHTY MAN, WAS MARRIED TO BATHSHEBA AND MURDERED BY DAVID.**
15. Who said, "You are the man"? **NATHAN**
16. Who was David's daughter who was raped? **TAMAR**
17. Who was Ahithophel? **A WISE COUNSELOR TO ABSALOM**
18. Who cursed David and threw rocks at him? **SHIMEI**
19. Which son of David tried to steal the throne from him? **ABSALOM**
20. Which books of the Bible describe the life of David? **1 AND 2 SAMUEL, 1 CHRONICLES, 1 KINGS**

ANSWERS

Quiz and answers courtesy of Brett Kreider.

Bible Quiz 99: The Long and Short of It

❶ Which is the longest chapter in the Bible? ____________________

❷ The shortest? ____

❸ How many verses does the longest chapter in the Bible have?

____

❹ What is the shortest verse in the English New Testament?

____

❺ Who lived the longest life in all of biblical history?

____

❻–❿ Can you name the five one-chapter books of the Bible? Hint: One is in the Old Testament, four are in the New Testament.

____

____

____

____

____

Answers to Bible Quiz 99: The Long and Short of It

1. Which is the longest chapter in the Bible? **PSALM 119**

2. The shortest? **PSALM 117**

3. How many verses does the longest chapter in the Bible have? **176**

4. What is the shortest verse in the English New Testament? **"JESUS WEPT"** (John 11:35)

5. Who lived the longest life in all of biblical history? **METHUSELAH**

6-10. Can you name the 5 one-chapter books of the Bible? Hint: One is in the Old Testament, four are in the New Testament.

OBADIAH, PHILEMON, 2 JOHN, 3 JOHN, JUDE

Bible Quiz 100: Tall and Short, Big and Small

1. Who was the famous giant of the Bible? ________________

2. How tall was he (approximately)?

❑ 7 ft. ❑ 8 ft. ❑ 9 ft. ❑ 10 ft.

3. Who killed him? ________________________________

4. What was the name of the tall brother of this man (the giant slayer)?

____

5. What was the name of the tall Israelite monarch who persecuted the giant slayer? ________________________________

6. Who was the "fat man" of the book of Judges? ________________

7. Who slew him? ________________________________

8. What was the name of the short man who climbed a tree to glimpse Jesus? ________________________________

9. In which Gospel do we read about his conversion? ______________

10. Who was the shortest man in the Bible? (This is a joke question!)

____

Answers to Bible Quiz 100: Tall and Short, Big and Small

1. Who was the famous giant of the Bible? **GOLIATH**

2. How tall was he (approximately)? **9 FEET (9"4")**

3. Who killed him? **DAVID**

4. What was the name of the tall brother of this man (the giant slayer)? **ELIAB**

5. What was the name of the tall Israelite monarch who persecuted the giant slayer? **SAUL**

6. Who was the "fat man" of the book of Judges? **EGLON**

7. Who slew him? **EHUD**

8. What was the name of the short man who climbed a tree to glimpse Jesus? **ZACCHAEUS**

9. In which gospel do we read about his conversion? **LUKE** (Chapter 19)

10. Who was the shortest man in the Bible? (This is a joke question!) **NEHEMIAH ("KNEE-HIGH-MIA")**. But there was one even shorter: **BILDAD THE SHUHITE (SHOE-HEIGHT)**. Can we top this? **THE PHILIPPIAN JAILER** (He slept on his "watch.")

When calculating your score, if you were stumped by question 10, give yourself credit!

Bible Quiz 101: The Beatitudes

❶ How many beatitudes are there in Matthew 5? ________________

❷ What is the reward for those who hunger and thirst after righteousness?

____

❸ Which other Gospel has a list of beatitudes? ________________

❹ Acts 20 contains one more dominical beatitude [a blessing uttered by the Lord]. What is it? ______________________________

❺ In Romans 4:7, Paul gives a beatitude (quoting Psalm 32): "Blessed are those whose transgressions ______________________________

______________________________."

❻-❿ Which book(s) of the Bible contain(s) the following five beatitudes?

A. Blessed is the one who reads the words of this prophecy… ________

B. Blessed are the dead who die in the Lord… ________________

C. Blessed are those who are invited to the wedding supper of the Lamb…

____

D. Blessed and holy are those who have part in the first resurrection…

____

E. Blessed are those who wash their robes… ________________

Answers to Bible Quiz 101: The Beatitudes

1. How many beatitudes are there in Matthew 5? **EIGHT**—including one double beatitude (the last one)

2. What is the reward for those who hunger and thirst after righteousness? **THEY WILL BE FILLED/SATISFIED**

3. Which other Gospel has a list of beatitudes? **LUKE** (Chapter 6)

4. Acts 20 contains one more dominical beatitude [a blessing uttered by the Lord]. What is it? **"IT IS MORE BLESSED TO GIVE THAN TO RECEIVE."**

5. In Romans 4:7, Paul gives a beatitude (quoting Psalm 32): "Blessed are those whose transgressions: **"ARE FORGIVEN"**

6-10. Which book(s) of the Bible contain(s) the following five beatitudes? **REVELATION (ALL 5!)**

A. Blessed is the one who reads the words of this prophecy… **CHAPTER 1**

B. Blessed are the dead who die in the Lord… **CHAPTER 14**

C. Blessed are those who are invited to the wedding supper of the Lamb... **CHAPTER 19**

D. Blessed and holy are those who have part in the first resurrection… **CHAPTER 20**

E. Blessed are those who wash their robes… **CHAPTER 22**

ANSWERS

Bible Quiz 102: Babies

❶ Which famous baby was thrown into the river? ________________

❷ Who found him there and had mercy on him? ________________

❸ In which town was the baby Jesus born? ________________

❹ Who ordered the slaughter of all baby boys up to the age of two residing in this locale? ________________

❺ What were the names of Jesus' mother and (legal) father? ________________

____

❻ Who is portrayed as a "baby" in the beginning of Ezekiel 16—kicking about and helpless? ________________

❼ Which biblical character was never a baby in the first place? ________________

____

❽ How did Jesus react when people brought babies to him to be blessed by him? ❑ He rebuked them. ❑ He welcomed them.

❑ He delegated the blessing to his disciples.

❾ What routinely happened to babies in times of famine in the Old Testament? ________________

❿ What were the occupations of Shiphrah and Puah (Exodus 1:15)?

____

Answers to Bible Quiz 102: Babies

1. Which famous baby was thrown into the river? **MOSES**

2. Who found him there and had mercy on him? **PHARAOH'S DAUGHTER**

3. In which town was the baby Jesus born? **BETHLEHEM**

4. Who ordered the slaughter of all baby boys up to the age of two residing in this locale? **HEROD THE GREAT** (He died in 4 B.C.)

5. What were the names of Jesus' mother and (legal) father? **MARY AND JOSEPH**

6. Who is portrayed as a "baby" in the beginning of Ezekiel 16—kicking about and helpless? **"UNFAITHFUL JERUSALEM"**

7. Which biblical character was never a baby in the first place? **ADAM**

8. How did Jesus react when people brought babies to him to be blessed by him? **HE WELCOMED THEM.**

9. What routinely happened to babies in times of famine in the Old Testament? **THEY WERE EATEN** (Leviticus 26:29, Deuteronomy 28:53-57, 2 Kings 6:28, Jeremiah 19:9, Ezekiel 5:10)

10. What were the occupations of Shiphrah and Puah (Exodus 1:15)? **[CHIEF] MIDWIVES**

Bible Quiz 103: Human Sacrifice

❶ Which pagan god of the Old Testament required human sacrifice?

____

❷ Of which nation was he the god? ____________________

❸ By which means were babies to be sacrificed? ____________

❹ Which Israelite king sacrificed his own son in this way?

____

❺ Which famous patriarch was (in the end) NOT required to sacrifice his son? ______________________________

❻ What was the name of the son? ____________________

❼ Which book of the Bible recounts this important episode, in a biblical story full of messianic overtones? ____________________

❽ In 2 Kings 3, which king, in battle against the Israelites, sacrificed his own son on the city walls? _________________________

❾ In which chapter of Leviticus are the Israelites are commanded not to sacrifice their children? ❑ 8 ❑ 18 ❑ 28

❿ In which location did the Jews routinely perform their child sacrifices?

____

Answers to Bible Quiz 103: Human Sacrifice

1. Which pagan god of the Old Testament required human sacrifice? **MOLECH**

2. Of which nation was he the god? **AMMON**

3. By which means were babies to be sacrificed? **BURNING IN THE FIRE**

4. Which Israelite king sacrificed his own son in this way? **MANASSEH**

5. Which famous patriarch was (in the end) NOT required to sacrifice his son? **ABRAHAM**

6. What was the name of the son? **ISAAC**

7. Which book of the Bible recounts this important episode, in a biblical story full of messianic overtones? **GENESIS**

8. In 2 Kings 3, which king, in battle against the Israelites, sacrificed his own son on the city walls? **THE KING OF MOAB**

9. In which chapter of Leviticus are the Israelites are commanded not to sacrifice their children? **18**

10. In which location did the Jews routinely perform their child sacrifices? **VALLEY OF BEN HINNOM** (Jeremiah 32:35)

Bible Quiz 104: Four Difficult Questions

❶ Who was Isaiah's son with a four-part name? (Literally it means "quick to the plunder, swift to the spoil," or "swift is the booty, speedy is the prey.")

❷ Two birthday celebrations—and only two—are mentioned in the Bible. Can you name the persons? Hint: There is one in each testament.

❸ How many fish did Peter and friends net in John 21?

❹ What happened to Sosthenes, the Corinthian synagogue ruler, after he was beaten by the anti-Christian mob (Acts 18:7)?

Answers to Bible Quiz 104: Four Difficult Questions

1. Who was Isaiah's son with a four-part name?

MAHER-SHALAL-HASH-BAZ (Isaiah 8:3)!

2. Two birthday celebrations—and only two—are mentioned in the Bible. Can you name the persons?

PHARAOH (Genesis 40:20) and **HEROD** (Matthew 14:6)

3. How many fish did Peter and friends net in John 21? **153** (And yes, many have tried to interpret the significance of this number!)

4. What happened to Sosthenes, the Corinthian synagogue ruler, after he was beaten by the anti-Christian mob (Acts 18:7)?

HE BECAME A CHRISTIAN HIMSELF! (1 Corinthians 1:1)

Bible Quiz 105: Miscellaneous Miscellaneous Questions

❶ The word "Bible" does not appear in the Bible: ❑ True or ❑ False?

❷ The word "church" does not appear in the Bible: ❑ True or ❑ False?

❸ First Century church buildings contained pews: ❑ True or ❑ False?

❹ Which book comes after Ezekiel? ______________________________

❺ Which book follows Philippians? ______________________________

❻ How many chapters are in the four gospels?

❑ 59 ❑ 89 ❑ 99 ❑ 209

❼ In which book do we read about Goliath, the Philistine giant?

____

❽ In which book do we read about Eglon, the "Jabba the Hutt" of the Old Testament? ____

❾ In which book do we read about Zacchaeus, the diminutive tax collector who responded so generously to the gospel? ____________________

❿ Most of the book of Job is poetry: ❑ True or ❑ False?

Answers to Bible Quiz 105: Miscellaneous Miscellaneous Questions

1. The word "Bible" does not appear in the Bible: **TRUE**

2. The word "church" does not appear in the Bible: **FALSE**

3. First century church buildings contained pews: **FALSE**

There were no custom built church buildings in the New Testament.

4. Which book comes after Ezekiel? **DANIEL**

5. Which book follows Philippians? **COLOSSIANS**

6. How many chapters are there in the four gospels? **89**

7. In which book do we read about Goliath, the Philistine giant? **1 SAMUEL**

8. In which book do we read about Eglon, the "Jabba the Hutt" of the Old Testament? **JUDGES**

9. In which book do we read about Zacchaeus, the diminutive tax collector who responded so generously to the gospel? **LUKE**

10. Most of the book of Job is primarily poetry: **TRUE**

Bible Quiz 106: The Cosmic Bible Quiz

TIME LIMIT: 40 MINUTES

Each question is worth one point, and all are multiple choice. Please write all your responses (by letter) in the space at margin. Guessing will not hurt you, it can only help. Check over your work carefully! Best of luck! – DJ

DIFFICULTY:

SECTION I: THE OLD TESTAMENT 9.5/10

SECTION II: THE NEW TESTAMENT 8.0/10

SECTION III: THEOLOGY 7.5/10

SECTION IV: BIBLE TRIVIA 9.0/10

SECTION I: THE OLD TESTAMENT

WARM-UP QUESTIONS

______ 1. What was the final book of the Hebrew Old Testament?
A. Malachi B. Chronicles C. Psalms

______ 2. How many books were there in the Hebrew Old Testament?
A. Thirty-nine B. Twenty-two C. Forty

______ 3. How many chapters does Ruth have?
A. Three B. Four C. Five

______ 4. How many years did Methuselah live?
A. 777 B. 919 C. 969

______ 5. The shortest chapter of the Old Testament is
A. Psalm 117 B. Jeremiah 45 C. Lamentations 5

VERSE IDENTIFICATION

_______ 6. "He will honor a god of fortresses; a god unknown to his fathers he will honor with gold and silver, with precious stones and costly gifts"?
A. Job 4:17 B. 2 Chronicles 11:17 C. Daniel 11:38 D. Malachi 5:38

_______ 7. "Woe to the city of blood, full of lies, full of plunder, never without victims!"
A. Ezekiel 40:2 B. Zechariah 2:2 C. Nahum 3:1 D. Habakkuk 2:78 E. Tobit 3:6

_______ 8. "He draws up the drops of water, which distill as rain to the streams."
A. Psalm 8:4 B. Job 36:27 C. Amos 4:9 D. Genesis 2:7 E. Leviticus 19:18

_______ 9. "...With a donkey's jawbone I have made donkeys of them. With a donkey's jawbone I have killed a thousand men."
A. Judges 15:16 B. 1 Samuel 12:12 C. 2 Samuel 17:32

_______ 10. "In the thirtieth year, in the fourth month on the fifth day, while I was among the exiles by the Kebar River, the heavens were opened and I saw visions of God."
A . Jeremiah 1:1 B. Ezekiel 1:1 C. Daniel 1:1 D. Joel 1:1

ARRANGE IN ORDER

_______ 11. i. Alexander the Great ii. Babylonian Exile iii. Exodus iv. Conquest
A. i-iii-iv-ii B . iii-iv-ii-i C. i-ii-iii-iv D. ii-i-iv-iii E. iv-iii-ii-i

_______ 12. i. Abraham ii. Ephraim iii. Joseph iv. Jacob v. Isaac
A. ii-iii-i-v-iv B. i-v-iv-iii-ii C. i-iv-v-iii-ii D. i-ii-iii-iv-v

_______ 13. i. Esther ii. Zephaniah iii. Amos iv. Job
A. ii-iv-iii-i B. i-iv-iii-ii C. i-ii-iii-iv D. iv-iii-ii-i

_______ 14. i. Gehazi ii. Melchizedek iii. Haggai iv. Jethro
A. ii-iv-i-iii B. i-ii-iii-iv C. iv-iii-ii-i D. ii-iii-i-iv

_______ 15. i. Assyria ii. Persia iii. Rome iv. Babylon v. Greece
A. iv-i-ii-v-iii B. i-iv-ii-v-iii C. v-iv-iii-ii-i

WARM-DOWN QUESTIONS

_______ 16. The Old Testament was written in which two languages?
A. Latin and Greek B. Greek and Hebrew C. Hebrew and Aramaic

_______ 17. Which book does not contain the lesser used of these two languages?
A. Genesis B. Ezra C. Daniel D. Job

_______ 18. Which of the following terms are virtual synonyms?
i. Pentateuch ii. Law iii. Torah iv. Books of Moses
A. i and iii B. ii and iii C. i, iii and iv D. i, ii, iii and iv

_______ 19. Which verse exhibits the names of God?
A. Genesis 33:2 B. Exodus 6:3 C. Leviticus 27:27 D. Numbers 4:4

_______ 20. Which two passages contain the Decalogue, or Ten Commandments?
A. Exodus 20 and 21 B. Deuteronomy 5 and 6
C. Exodus 20 and Deuteronomy 5 D. Exodus 20 and Deuteronomy 6

_______ 21. Which two sons of Aaron were struck down?
A. Nahu and Abidab B. Uz and Buz C. Kenan and Konan D. Nadab and Abihu

_____ 22. How many censuses are taken in Numbers?
A. One B. Two C. Three

_____ 23. How many chapters are there in the Law?
A. 155 B. 187 C. 205 D. 333

_____ 24. In the Creation account, which day of preparation is paired theologically with Day 5? (The day when we see God's providence)
A. Day 1 B. Day 2 C. Day 3 D. Day 7

_____ 25. About how many years ago did Abram live?
A. 2000 B. 3000 C. 4000

SECTION II: THE NEW TESTAMENT

WARM-UP QUESTIONS

_____ 26. Who wrote Acts?
A. Mark B. Priscilla C. Luke D. Peter

_____ 27. How many letters are in the New Testament, excluding Acts and Revelation?
A. 12 B. 18 C. 20 D. 21 E. 23

_____ 28. Where was Paul shipwrecked?
A. Rome B. Malta C. Cyprus D. Cos

_____ 29. The New Testament documents were written:
A. In the Dark Ages by monks
B. By Nostradamus & Co.
C. In the first century by eyewitnesses
D. On one of Paul's pilgrimages to India

_____ 30. How many chapters are there in the gospels?
A. 89 B. 91 C. 93 D. 99

_____ 31. The New Testament was written in: A. Latin B. Greek C. Sanskrit

_____ 32. A specimen of this language is:
A. Εν αρχη ην ο λογος
B. Et creavit Deus hominem
C. Haben Sie ein Dachshund?
D. Бог создал землю.

_____ 33. How many chapters are there in Hebrews?
A. 10 B. 12 C. 13 D. 15

_____ 34. What was Cornelius' rank? A. Decurion B. Centurion C. Imperator

_____ 35. The oldest surviving New Testament manuscript is located in:
A. Jerusalem B. Manchester C. Amman D. Cairo E. Tel Aviv

LIFE OF JESUS

_____ 36. How old was Jesus when he began his ministry?
A. Twelve B. Twenty C. Thirty D. Forty E. About thirty

_____ 37. What does "Jesus" mean? A. Victory B. Salvation C. Messiah

_____ 38. What is the Old Testament (Hebraic) form of Jesus?
A. Jacob B. Joshua C. Jehovah D. Jeshurun

_____ 39. In which Gospel do Magi visit the infant Jesus?
A. Matthew B. Mark C. Luke

_____ 40. Who was the "King of the Jews" when Jesus was born?
A. Nero B. Herod C. George III D. Tutankhamun

_____ 41. How many half-brothers did Jesus have?
A. None B. Two C. Four D. Six

_____ 42. Which verse shows us that Jesus never used miraculous powers before his official ministry began?
A. John 2:11 B. Luke 2:11 C. Mark 2:11 D. Matthew 2:11

_____ 43. Literal words of Jesus can be found in how many books of the NT?
A. Four B. Five C. Six D. Seven E. Eight

_____ 44. Into whose hands did Jesus entrust his mother while on the cross?
A. Zebedee's son B. Zacchaeus' mother C. Herod's step-daughter

_____ 45. In how many Gospels is the feeding of the five thousand found?
A. Only one B. Two C. Three D. All four

_____ 46. Which OT Psalm of faith did Jesus quote from the cross?
A. Psalm 23 B. Psalm 22 C. Psalm 115 D. Psalm 2

_____ 47. Jesus' genealogy is found in: A. Matthew 1 and Luke 1
B. Matthew 1 and Luke 3 C. Luke 1 and Matthew 3 D. Luke 3 and Matthew 3

_____ 48. Which biography of Jesus is shortest?
A. Matthew B. Mark C. Luke D. John

_____ 49. In which chapter of Matthew did Jesus scold the Pharisees?
A. Eleven B. Twenty-one C. Twenty-three D. Twenty-five

_____ 50. During how long a period did Jesus appear to his disciples following his Resurrection?
A. 8 days B. 10 days C. 40 days D. 50 days

WARM-DOWN QUESTIONS

_____ 51. Which book prophesies the downfall of the Roman Empire?
A. Matthew B. Acts C. Jude D. Revelation

_____ 52. Which two New Testament books have the most in common?
A. 1 Thessalonians and Colossians B. 1 Peter and 1 John C. 2 Peter and Jude
D. 1 Timothy and Mark

_____ 53. Which is the shortest book in the NT (number of words in Greek)?
A. 2 John B. 3 John

_____ 54. Which museum contains the Codex Alexandrinus and Sinaiticus?
A. Vatican B. British C. Louvre D. Imperial War Museum

_____ 55. Which is longer, the New Testament or the Koran?
A. The New Testament B. The Koran

SECTION III: THEOLOGY

_____ 56. Purgatory, though nowhere found in the Bible, is found in the:
A. Pseudepigrapha B. Apocrypha C. Nicene Creed D. Magna Carta

_____ 57. Ecclesiology is the study of the:
A. Martyrs B. Church C. Clergy

_____ 58. Soteriology is the study of:
A. Salvation B. Sacred music C. Clergy D. Martyrs

_____ 59. The fourth word of the ("fish") acronym ICHTHUS is:
A. Lord B. Son C. Savior D. Devotion

_____ 60. All the following English Bibles preceded the 1611 KJV except:
A. Tyndale B. Coverdale C. Confraternity D. Broad E. Matthew

_____ 61. The Petrine epistles number:
A. Two B. Three C. Four

_____ 62. Which "Pauline" epistle is not written by Paul?
A. James B. Hebrews C. Titus D. Galatians

_____ 63. How many Pastoral epistles are there?
A. Two B. Three C. Four

_____ 64. During the last century, most liberal scholars dated the writing of the NT documents to which century?
A. First B. Second C. Third D. Later

_____ 65. Theology literally is the study of:
A. God B. Religion C. Faith D. Belief E. Church

_____ 66. The defense of the Christian faith is known as:
A. Polemics B. Vitriolics C. Apologetics D. Humiletics

_____ 67. The monastic movement gathered strength in which century?
A. First B. Second C. Third D. Twelfth

_____ 68. The term gnosticism comes from the word for:
A. Mysticism B. Knowledge C. Diagnostics

_____ 69. Docetists denied that Jesus had a:
A. Physical body B. Immortal soul C. Navel D. Conscience

_____ 70. Which of the following is not a monotheistic religion?
A. Judaism B. Islam C. Hinduism D. Zoroastrianism

_____ 71. Which verse says that we were baptized by the Holy Spirit?
A. Acts 2:5 B. Acts 2:38 C. 1 Corinthians 12:13 D. Ephesians 4:5

_____ 72. Which verse clearly refutes the notion of Original Sin?
A. Jeremiah 18:20 B. Ezekiel 18:20 C. Daniel 18:20 D. Matthew 18:20

_____ 73. The tetragrammaton has reference to the:
A. Four letters of Paul written in 55 A.D. B. Four doctrines of heretics after 100 A.D. C. Divine name D. Resurrection

_____ 74. Sikhism was founded by:
A. Mahavira B. Nanak C. Lao Tse D. Zoroaster

_____ 75. The Apocrypha were added to Catholic Bibles in which Council?
A. Vatican II B. Trent C. Fourth Lateran D. Constantinople

SECTION IV: BIBLE TRIVIA

_____ 76. Which is the shortest verse in the English Bible?
A. Luke 17:32 B. John 11:25 C. John 11:35 D . Revelation 1:1

_____ 77. Who irreverently tried to steady the Ark?
A. Uzzah B. Urim C. Uri

_____ 78. Clean animals boarded the ark in:
A. Twos B. Sevens C. Fours D. April, 3106 B.C.

_____ 79. Who first got drunk in the Bible?
A. Noah B. Belshazzar C. Peter D. Herod Agrippa I

_____ 80. The word bible comes from the Greek word for:
A. Holy B. Book C. Scroll D. Double-edged

_____ 81. Approximately how many chapters does the Bible have?
A. 800 B. 1000 C. 1100 D. 1500 E. 1700

_____ 82. Titus ministered on the island of:
A. Cyprus B. Crete C. Cos D. Rhodes

_____ 83. Clement records that after release from a Roman prison, Paul reached:
A. The "Pillars of Hercules" (Spain) B. The Philippine Islands
C. North America D. Umtata, Transkei

_____ 84. The Tower of Babel is found in which chapter of Genesis?
A. Eight B. Eleven C. Fifty-two D. Sixty-six

_____ 85. Diagnosis of leprosy is found in which book of the Law?
A. Exodus B. Leviticus C. Numbers D. Deuteronomy

_____ 86. Daniel was written around: A. 800 B.C. B. 530 B.C. C. 400 B.C.

_____ 87. Goliath stood how tall? A. 9'4" B. 9'9" C. 10'10"

_____ 88. What is the last word of the Bible?
A. God B. Amen C. Forever D. Quickly E. Book

_____ 89. Felix was succeeded by: A. Festus B. Agrippa C. Porcius D. Drusilla

_____ 90. Haggai's contemporary prophet (in 520 B.C.) was:
A. Zephaniah B. Zechariah C. Micaiah D. Obadiah E. Jeremiah

_____ 91. How many people were baptized at Pentecost?
A. 1,500 B. 3,000 C. 5,000

_____ 92. How much of Proverbs was written by Solomon?
A. All B. Most C. Some D. None

_____ 93. Who prophesied between 626 and 587 B.C.?
A. Isaiah B. Jeremiah C. Ezekiel D. Daniel

_____ 94. Who lived longer, Abraham or Job?
A. Abraham B. Job

_____ 95. How many books in the Bible have 28 chapters?
A. One B. Two C. Four

SUPER-HARD BIBLE QUESTIONS

_____ 96. Wormwood is found in Jeremiah, Lamentations, Revelation, Proverbs and:
A. Amos B. Revelation C. 3 Chronicles D. Psalms

_____ 97. Who is the "anointed" in Isaiah 45:1?
A. Jesus B. Cyrus C. Isaiah D. Daniel E. Yahweh

_____ 98. "Waydabber YHWH el-moshe bemidhbar" is the beginning of which book? Hint: the word "bemidhbar" means in the desert.
A. Galatians B. Ephesians C. Numbers D. Lamentations E. Mark

_____ 99. The words Egypt, Egyptians and forms thereof occur in the Bible approximately:
A. 100 times B. 200 times C. 400 times D. 800 times E. 1,600 times

_____ 100. A hapax, from the Greek word for once, is a word occurring only one time in a document or book. Which hapax occurs in Romans 16:1?
A. Cenchreae B. Envelope C. Commend D. Walnut
E. Phoebe F. Aardvark G. Procrastinate H. Cosmic

Congratulations! You have completed the Cosmic Bible Quiz!

Answers to the Cosmic Bible Quiz:

1-10	B B B C A C C B A B	**51-60**	D C B B A B B A B C
11-20	B B D A B C D D B C	**61-70**	A B B B A C C B A C
21-30	D B B B C C D B C A	**71-80**	C B C B B C A B A B
31-40	B A C B B E B B A B	**81-90**	C B A B B B A B A B
41-50	C A E A D B B B C C	**91-100**	B B B B B A B C D E

Score:

0-40	Keep studying!
41-60	Average
61-80	Good
81-90	Very good
91-100	Excellent

How did you do? Most Christians taking the test score around 50 points, though a number of the better Bible students have scored in the 90s.

Bible Quiz 107: The Old Testament

See how long it takes you to complete the quiz. Each period of history has four Bible questions, moving from easier to harder. You are racing against yourself.

❶ Genesis
A. What is the last word in Genesis? ______________________
B. Who married Rebekah? ______________________
C. In which chapter does Joseph flee Potiphar's wife? ____________
D. In which chapter do we read about Judah and Tamar? ____________

❷ The Law: Exodus-Deuteronomy
A. From which country did the Exodus take place? What is the name of the man who ruled this country? __________
B. Add up the number of chapters in Exodus, Leviticus, Numbers and Deuteronomy. What's the total? ______________________
C. In which two chapters do we find the Ten Commandments? ____________
D. Where do we read of the punishment of Nadab and Abihu? ____________

❸ Conquest: Joshua
A. What does God tell Joshua to do in Joshua 1:8? ______________
B. In which chapter do we find Rahab? ______________________
C. Who was Achan's father? ______________________
D. Which came first, the southern conquest or the northern conquest? __________

❹ Judges: Judges, Ruth, 1 Samuel
A. In which chapter do we first read of Samson? ______________
B. Who was the last judge in the period of the Judges? ____________
C. What happened to Adoni-Bezek's big toes? ______________
D. Where do we find the Song of Deborah? ______________________

❺ Kings: 1-2 Samuel, Kings, Chronicles
A. Who was the first king of Israel? ______________________
B. Who was the king in whose time Israel split into two kingdoms? __________
C. How long did Manasseh reign? ______________________
D. How many chapters are there in 1-2 Samuel combined? ____________

❻ Exile: Ezra-Nehemiah, Esther, Daniel

A. Who adopted Esther? ____________

B. What was Daniel's (new) Babylonian name? ____________

C. The first paragraph of Ezra is like the last paragraph of which other book?

____

D. The four kingdoms of Daniel 7 are also referred to in which other chapter of Daniel? ____________

❼ Psalms

A. What does Psalm 150 keep saying over and over? ____________

B. What is the first chapter of each of the 5 "books" of Psalms? ____________

C. Which Psalm did Moses write? ____________

D. Which Psalm ends by saying, "The darkness is my closest friend"? Hint: This Psalm is in Book III of Psalms. ____________

❽ Wisdom: Job, Proverbs, Ecclesiastes, Song of Solomon

A. Does Job's wife have a name? ____________

B. Which proverb in chapter 16 is identical to Proverbs 14:12? ____________

C. What is the beginning of Ecclesiastes talking about? ____________

D. Who were the other two companions of Eliphaz? ____________

❾ Prophets: Isaiah-Malachi

A. Which book, written by a prophet, has exactly 52 chapters? ____________

B. How many books are written by "Minor Prophets"? ____________

C. Where in the NT is the last verse of Isaiah quoted? ____________

D. Which NT book makes an allusion to Ezekiel 38? ____________

❿ Old Testament (General)

A. What is the last Old Testament book? ____________

B. What is the shortest Old Testament book? ____________

C. What is the parallel chapter to 2 Samuel 24? Hint: It is somewhere in the Chronicles. ____________

D. Which two Old Testament passages contain "the greatest commandment" and "the second greatest"? ____________

Answers and Scoring for Old and New Testament Speed Quizzes:

Answers will not be supplied for this quiz. Learn by finding your own answers!

Bible Quiz 108: The New Testament

Again, record how long it takes you to complete the following quiz.

❶ Gospels
A. Which Gospel contains the Sermon on the Mount? ____________________
B. How many chapters are there in Mark? ____________________
C. Which Gospel writer recounts the Emmaus Road incident? ____________________
D. In how many of the Gospels do we find the feeding of the 5000? __________

❷ Acts
A. Who said, "Repent and be baptized"? ____________________
B. On what island were Paul and company shipwrecked?____________________
C. Where is Paul at the end of the book of Acts? ____________________
D. Who wrote Acts? ____________________

❸ Letters of Paul
A. Paul wrote Romans: True or False? ____________________
B. Which is the shortest of Paul's letters? ____________________
C. Galatians 2:11 reads, "I opposed him to his face, because he was in the wrong." This verse is speaking about Paul and ____________________.
D. Which two letters focus the most on grace and works? ____________________

❹ Hebrews
A. Does Hebrews indicate its author? ____________________
B. "Without faith, it is impossible to ____________________."
C. Which chapter focuses on angels? ____________________
D. Which chapter mentions milk and meat? ____________________

❺ Letter of James
A. In chapter 1, the Word is compared to a ____________________; hopefully, we will not look into it, walk away and forget what we see.
B. Which book of the Bible comes immediately after James? ______________
C. Confessing sins is mentioned in the last chapter of James: ❑ True or ❑ False?
D. Which chapter contains these words: "Let your yes be yes…"? __________

❻ Letters of Peter
A. How many letters of Peter are there? ____________________
B. Which chapter of 1 Peter says bluntly, "baptism saves you"? __________
C. In which chapter of 2 Peter does the apostle frankly admit that Paul's letters contain some things hard to understand? ____________________

D. In which chapter of 1 Peter does the apostle advise wives how to win over their non-believing husbands? ______________________

❼ Letters of John

A. How many letters of John are there? ______________________

B. If anyone denies that Jesus came in the flesh, according to 2 John, such a person is a deceiver and the "__________." Hint: the answer begins with an "'A."

C. Which other two NT books is John thought to have penned? ______________

D. In which letter do we read of Diotrephes and Demetrius? ______________

❽ Letter of Jude

A. How many verses does Jude have? ❑ 15 ❑ 25 ❑ 45 ❑ 105

B. Jude refers to Enoch: ❑ True or ❑ False?

C. Jude refers to the ancient cities of S ______________and G ____________.

D. The content of Jude is most similar to: ❑ 2 Corinthians ❑ 2 Peter ❑ 2 John

❾ Revelation

A. Revelation contain hundreds of allusions to the O ________ T __________.

B. On which island was the author of Revelation living (really, exiled)? ________

C. Which chapter tells that the saints overcome by the word of God and the word of their testimony? ______________________

D. What is the alternative name for this book?

❑ The Apostrophe ❑ The Apocalypse ❑ The Apotheosis

❿ New Testament (General)

A. How many books are there in the New Testament? ______________

B. The longest and shortest NT books are L ___________and 2 ____________

C. How many NT books begin with the letter "M"? ______________

D. Can you arrange the following books in chronological order?

___ 1 Timothy ___ 1 Thessalonians ____ 2 Timothy ____Romans

Answers and Scoring for Old and New Testament Speed Quizzes:

Answers will not be supplied for this quiz. Learn by finding your own answers!

Time:	5-10 minutes	You know your Bible well.
	11-15 minutes	Good.
	16-20 minutes	Fair.
	21 plus minutes	Needs improvement.

DOUGLAS A. JACOBY
A Quick Overview of the
BIBLE
Understanding How All the
Pieces Fit Together

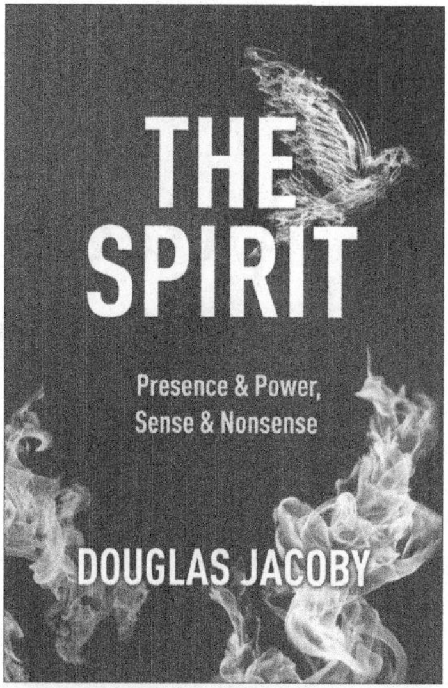
THE
SPIRIT
Presence & Power,
Sense & Nonsense
DOUGLAS JACOBY

The Radical Life of Elijah
Chariots
of Fire
Dr. Douglas Jacoby

An Evangelism Handbook
for the 21st Century
Till the
NETS
Are Full
DOUGLAS JACOBY

Made in the USA
Coppell, TX
16 March 2026

73977578R00128